Linda Nesvisky

JEWISH
Philadelphia

JEWISH
Philadelphia
A GUIDE TO ITS
Sights & Stories

LINDA NESVISKY

Charleston London

THE
History
PRESS

Published by The History Press
Charleston, SC 29403
www.historypress.net

Cover: *Religious Liberty* by sculptor Sir Moses Ezekiel, commissioned by B'nai B'rith
for the American Centennial. *Photograph by Ben Sutherland.*

First published 2010

Manufactured in the United States

ISBN 978.1.59629.903.0

Nesvisky, Linda.
Jewish Philadelphia : a guide to its sights and stories / Linda Nesvisky.
p. cm.
Includes bibliographical references and index.
ISBN 978-1-59629-903-0
1. Jews--Pennsylvania--Philadelphia--History. 2. Historic sites--Pennsylvania--
Philadelphia--Guidebooks. 3. Walking--Pennsylvania--Philadelphia--Guidebooks.
4. Philadelphia (Pa.)--Buildings, structures, etc.--Guidebooks. 5. Philadelphia
(Pa.)--Guidebooks. I. Title.
F158.9.J5N47 2010
974.8'11--dc22
2010003360

For Carmel, Leon, Alma, Tevah, Tali and Eden.

Contents

CONTENTS

ACKNOWLEDGEMENTS

I am grateful to all those who willingly gave of their time in helping me to write this book. Several are acknowledged within the text, but I also benefited greatly from the assistance of Stuart Appel, Lynne Balaban, Norm Brody, J. Lee Deddens, Karie Diethorn, Frank Eidmann, Judah Ferst, Claudia Fisher, Nina Fisher, Howard Fishman, Harvey Friedrich, Rabbi Albert Gabbai, Rabbi David Glanzman-Krainin, Judy Golden, Ruth Kapp Hartz, Jim Hauser, Professor Joel Hecker, Donna Katz, Lou Kessler, Cornelia King, Rebecca Levine, Anne McLaughlin, Myrna Merbeck, Christopher Mulvey, William Novak, Beth Peckman, Alex Podmaski, Rita Poley, Claire Rechnitzer, Rabbi Haim Rechnitzer, Mickie Rosen, Martin Jay Rosenblum, Karen Schoenewaldt, Joseph Smuckler, Rabbi Lance Sussman, Ellen Tilman and, oh yes, my husband Matt. Lastly I want to thank The History Press for its guidance and encouragement.

INTRODUCTION

It's widely agreed that the capital of Jewish America is New York City. That may be true today, but it wasn't always so—no more than Washington, D.C., was always the capital of the United States. You know, of course, that the original capital city of this great country was Philadelphia, the very place in which the whole notion of independence and a federal union of the colonies was designed and hammered out. Well, in many respects, the story of Jewish America was formed right along with the new nation—right here in the City of Brotherly Love.

Philadelphia remains one of the centers of Jewish life in America. According to a recent census ("Jewish Population Study of Greater Philadelphia") commissioned by the Jewish Federation in 2009, there are 215,000 Jews residing in the greater metropolitan area. Equally significant, Philadelphia is home to some of the nation's greatest American Jewish institutions, with special value for historians, researchers and genealogists (take that, New York!). But even Jewish Philadelphians may not always be aware of the history of their forefathers in this city, how and why they came here and the impact they and Jewish thinking had on the founding of the new nation.

In this regard it's no accident that the National Museum of American Jewish History is located in Philadelphia and not in New

A bird's-eye view of Philadelphia.

York or Washington or Los Angeles. It is entirely appropriate that the museum is just a few steps from the church in which George Washington worshipped, the building in which the Declaration of Independence was drafted and the chambers in which the U.S. Congress first assembled. That's because both the United States and the American Jewish story were essentially established on the same ground—on the same cobblestoned streets and alongside the same riverfronts.

Yet this is history too little known, and that's why this book was written—to highlight for visitors (and natives) some fascinating stories about Jews and Philadelphia.

So get ready to enjoy some history, some biography, some art and some culture. (Don't worry, I'll also tell you where you can get a good nosh.) Then come take a walk for an hour or two. This book will help you see where so much important history occurred, both Jewish and American. Along the way, we'll share some fascinating stories and hear about some outstanding individuals and some astonishing ideas.

A note on the book's organization: First I offer you ten snapshot vignettes concerning the most important sites and institutions in the Greater Philadelphia area. Then, for our walking tour, I've selected nine of the most significant central locations regarding Jewish history in colonial Philadelphia. Our stops are based on the walking tours that I've been leading since the formation of ShalomPhillyTours in 2005. I created those tours because, after guiding in Philadelphia for some twenty years, I felt that not enough Jewish history was being covered here. I also include information on the brand-new National Jewish American History Museum on Independence Mall.

Part I

PERSONALITIES, PLACES, RESOURCES

THE HOLOCAUST MEMORIAL ON THE PARKWAY

Ask sculptors when it became apparent to them that three-dimensional art would be their chosen form of expression, and almost to a person they will answer that it was realized from a young age. This was the case with Nathan Rapoport, the creator of *Monument to the Six Million Martyrs*, located on the magnificent Benjamin Franklin Parkway. Rapoport decided to be a sculptor by the age of fifteen. But life's unhappy experiences made him dedicate himself to memorializing the Holocaust. This was his sole theme. His monumental sculptures are located throughout the world. Philadelphia's is the first Holocaust memorial sculpture in North America. Michael Kimmelman, art critic of the *New York Times*, summarizes Rapoport as a "realist sculptor of dead and battling Jews."

Rapoport was born in Warsaw in 1911. In 1936, he was offered the opportunity to study in France and Italy but opted for the Soviet Union when the Soviets invaded Poland. In Russia, he acquired a studio and began creating Soviet-style sculptures. He developed his socialist realism style during this time and continued to work in the official style of the Soviet Union until his death.

At war's end, he returned to his native city to study art at the Warsaw Academy of Fine Art. As a Polish citizen he was entitled to a free college education. Still, Rapoport had to have been a

Holocaust Memorial on the Ben Franklin Parkway. *Jewish Federation of Greater Philadelphia.*

determined student to contemplate returning to the graveyard of Poland. Indeed, when his studies were completed in 1950, he immigrated to the United States—but not before erecting his first monumental sculpture, *Wall of Remembrance*, in 1948 in the ruins of the Warsaw Ghetto.

Rapoport was eventually commissioned by the State of Israel to create the monument to Mordechai Anilewicz at Kibbutz Yad Mordechai. Anilewicz was the leader of the Warsaw Ghetto uprising. Another commission allowed Rapoport to create *The Last March* for the Yad Vashem Holocaust Museum and Memorial in Jerusalem. A Rapoport sculpture in New York City's Liberty State Park in the Battery is of a GI carrying a concentration camp inmate to freedom.

Philadelphia's *Monument to the Six Million Martyrs* is located at the beginning of the Ben Franklin Parkway at Sixteenth Street, one block north of City Hall. It was made in Italy and installed in 1964. On Holocaust Remembrance Day, hundreds gather here for a memorial service.

The sculpture depicts men, women and children intertwined with flames swirling upward to resemble a menorah at the top. The intertwining of limbs also suggests the burning bush (Exodus 3:2). The style of this sculpture recalls elements of sculptors Jacques Lipchitz and Auguste Rodin, both friends of Rapoport and both having works only blocks from each other very nearby.

A plan is in the works to significantly enhance the Holocaust Memorial site. The Philadelphia Holocaust Remembrance Foundation is working with Israeli architect Moshe Safdie to create the Holocaust Memorial Foundation's Center for Human Rights Education. Over $3 million has been raised toward this goal. The Philadelphia City Council also plans an educational facility to boost the prominence of the memorial, with an audiovisual center. This new center is supported by the Commonwealth of Pennsylvania, the City of Philadelphia and the Fairmont Park Commission.

The Jewish Community Relations Council (JCRC) of the Jewish Federation of Greater Philadelphia is in charge of the annual Holocaust Remembrance Day event, usually occurring in May. Adam Kessler is the director of JCRC and can be reached at akessler@jfgp.org.

Architect's digital rendering of the Holocaust Memorial Foundation's Center for Human Rights Education alongside the Memorial Sculpture on the Benjamin Franklin Parkway. *Moshe Safdie Associates.*

The Benjamin Franklin Parkway is often referred to as our city's cultural mile to distinguish it from the historical mile around Independence Hall area. The Parkway houses the Philadelphia Museum of Art, the Franklin Institute, the Philadelphia Free Library, the Rodin Museum and, soon, the Barnes Museum. The Parkway was begun in 1916. Paul Cret prepared the original plan. When William Penn planned our city in 1682, it was a grid. The Parkway is Philadelphia's only diagonal boulevard—a major deviation of that plan. This idea came about when the "City Beautiful" movement began to sweep the nation following Chicago's World Columbian Exposition of 1894. Its ideology promoted spacious expanses and monumental grandeur in the modern city.

Beaux Arts was the style of the time, and Philadelphia's Parkway Commission felt that a diagonal element in our city was a dynamic way to introduce and promote this avant-garde thinking. The Parkway has two boulevards separated by trees and a green belt, as well as two monumental fountains. It was modeled after the Champs-Élysées in Paris, with flags from every country displayed along its length in alphabetical order. But because the Holocaust Memorial stands at the beginning of the Parkway, the Israeli flag is the first in the parade of flags. It is a fine setting for Rapoport's memorial sculpture.

The Parkway begins at Love Park behind City Hall and terminates at the steps of the Museum of Art. The museum landing commands an excellent view of Philadelphia's skyline. Stand in the center of the landing to view it properly and then look down for the embedded footprints of "Rocky," the Sylvester Stallone boxing hero. This site is almost as popular with tourists as Independence Hall.

THE ROSENBACH MUSEUM AND LIBRARY: THE JEWEL IN THE CROWN

The Rosenbach (pronounced *Roe-sen-back*) Museum and Library is a welcoming and unique treasure in Philadelphia. Though off the beaten tourist path, at 2008–2010 Delancey Place, it is within walking distance of the "historic mile" area. It is easily accessible by bus no. 17 running westward along Market Street. It is a short walk from the Mikveh Israel Cemetery located on Ninth and Spruce Streets. Walk west along Spruce Street, and Delancey is a quick left turn between Spruce and Pine. The area is Society Hill, one of the two earliest neighborhoods in Philadelphia. Charming eighteenth-century homes dot narrow scenic lanes, and horse-drawn carriages help to set the scene back to the colonial and federal periods.

The museum was home to two brothers. Dr. A.S.W. Rosenbach (1876–1952) collected books and rare manuscripts, including Judaica. His business-savvy brother Philip (1863–1953) collected rare prints, drawings, paintings and antique furniture. The love of books and manuscripts was ignited for A.S.W. while he was working in Uncle Mo's (Moses Polock) bookstore. A.S.W. became so skilled at collecting that other collectors and institutions, such as the British Museum, feared his determination. Once he set his heart on something to add to his collection, he customarily outbid all competitors. But both brothers contributed toward making this museum and library a special place.

Newly restored, this outstanding residence was designed by the leading Philadelphia architect of the time, Frank Furness. Its beauty, along with the brothers' prized collections, combined to place the Rosenbach Museum and Library on the National Register of Historic Places. It has a welcoming back garden and outstanding furniture collection. The Rosenbach moreover is a research institution. It hosts literary conferences, has many guided tours and topical tours and offers varying exhibitions. Look for the town house with an American flag and walk in. Visiting hours are in a state of flux at the moment due to budget constraints, so it is best to check www.rosenbach.org or call 215-732-1600.

The dark wooden cabinet by the entrance belonged to Herman Melville and is filled with his books. Directly opposite the visitor's desk is the Sendak Gallery. A great children's storyteller and book illustrator (*Where the Wild Things Are* and more), Maurice Sendak donated to the Rosenbach in the early 1970s nearly ten thousand illustrations, manuscripts and ephemera to be enjoyed by visitors of all ages.

It all began when the writer journeyed from New York to Philadelphia's Free Library in 1966 to give a lecture. There he met the director of the Rosenbach and learned that they shared a love of Herman Melville. An excited Sendak rushed to the museum to see the original manuscripts of *Moby Dick* and other Melville writings. Sendak had been reading Melville since his early twenties and had even illustrated Melville's biography with thirty full-page ink and watercolor drawings.

Other items in the Rosenbach collection excited Sendak as well, such as the William Blake drawings and Lewis Carroll's original *Alice in Wonderland* novel with its John Tenniel drawings. (A.S.W. had outbid the British Museum for the copy that Carroll had presented to Alice Liddell, the model for the child in the story.) Then Sendak entered the Marianne Moore Room. The poet had been his neighbor and good friend in New York's Lower East Side. How nice it would be, he thought, to be neighbors again. In short, Sendak valued the Rosenbach Collection so highly that he persuaded the institution to include his works.

But we're not done yet. The museum actually owns James Joyce's handwritten manuscript of *Ulysses*. To commemorate the great Irish writer, the work is read aloud in its entirety each "Bloomsday" (June 16) by notable Philadelphians, actors, writers and others on the steps of the museum. And to celebrate the museum's Bram Stoker Collection, a Dracula Festival is held at the Rosenbach each October with a month-long series of events. Still more manuscripts and first editions by such authors as Oscar Wilde, Arthur Conan Doyle, Joseph Conrad and Dylan Thomas may be seen at the Rosenbach. The museum also has the only extant first edition (1733) of Benjamin Franklin's *Poor Richard's Almanack*, over one hundred letters written by George Washington and over two hundred letters by Abraham Lincoln.

Now for the Jewish connection: Via a fortuitous family relationship, the Rosenbach brothers amassed the furniture and writings of the descendants of Michael and Miriam Gratz,

The parlor room of the Rosenbach Museum and Library. *Rosenbach Museum and Library.*

founders of the great Jewish Philadelphia family. The Gratzes had twelve children, ten of whom survived to adulthood. All of the children were civic leaders during Philadelphia's federal period and were known for their philanthropy. (The Gratzes are discussed in the Walking Tour sections on the Mikveh Israel Synagogue and Mikveh Israel Cemetery.) Meanwhile, Aaron Levy, a business partner of Michael Gratz, had no children. Needing an heir, Levy adopted his friend's son Simon, to whom he left his estate. This adoption made the Rosenbach brothers related to the Gratz clan, because their mother Isabella was the great-niece of Aaron Levy.

The relationship was instrumental in the Rosenbachs' purchasing some of the furniture and paintings now seen in the Salon Room, directly behind the museum's front desk lobby. Portraits of some of the Gratz family members, by the noted artist Thomas Sully and his equally talented daughter Jane, are displayed here. One can view patriarch Michael's stern gaze directed toward his two beautiful daughters, Rebecca and Rachel. I was immediately drawn to the graceful portrait of Rebecca,

Portrait of Rebecca Gratz. *Rosenbach Museum and Library.*

likening it to a Jewish *Mona Lisa*, an association brought to mind by her hint of a smile and eyes that follow the viewer no matter where he is positioned.

Perhaps the jewel in the crown included in the rare book collection is the 1640 "Bay Psalm Book," named for the Massachusetts Bay Colony and the first book printed in what is now the United States. Hebrew type makes its first appearance in the Western hemisphere here. Only eleven copies are known to exist. Its proper title is *The Whole Book of Psalms*, and the work is a metrical rendition of the Psalms into English.

Archivist Elizabeth Fuller led me to the rare book room to view the Judaic collection of numerous Haggadahs and Hebrew Bibles. She unlocked some cases, wearing white cotton gloves, to show me some incunabula, which means printed editions from the 1500s. We both marveled over the Hebrew font. Vowels were printed under the text. Letters came in varying sizes and widths to justify the margins. It was ingenious! The range of characters could easily compete with those of the Chinese alphabet, especially in the Talmud, with its text, subtext and sub-subtext.

One of the most notable exhibits at the Rosenbach, Chosen, was held in 2008 and contained items selected from the rich Jewish resources in our city and showed a diversity of languages, from Chaldean to Yiddish. The exhibit was curated by David Stern, University of Pennsylvania Ruth Meltzer Professor of Classical History, and by Judith Guston, Rosenbach Museum and library curator and director of collections. The exhibit featured what Stern calls Philadelphia's "diaspora of Jewish books." Shown were sixty books, scrolls and related objects from the Mikveh Israel, Rodef Shalom and Keneseth Israel congregations, the Free Library of Philadelphia, the Haverford College Library, the Jewish Studies Program at the University of Pennsylvania, the Bryn Mawr College Library and the Rosenbach.

Among the exhibits were an eleventh-century Haggadah, the first Hebrew prayer book written for popular use, and the first known illustration depicting a bar mitzvah. The exhibition title, Chosen, referred to the rich heritage of the "People of the Book." I asked David Stern to comment on this incredible exhibit. He wrote:

> *Places sometimes hold promises one can never even imagine. I have lived in Philadelphia for more than 25 years. Over the last 12 years my scholarly research has centered upon the Jewish book as a physical object—what it looks like, what it meant for a Jew to hold such a book in his hands, how these books themselves had lives. The more one works on books, one realizes that they are very much like people. And Jewish books are like Jews. They wander, are exiled, are miraculously saved (and sometimes destroyed) but always there's a story.*
>
> *Over the course of my research I began to discover, in various public collections in the greater Philadelphia area, in university libraries, public libraries, synagogues, even Christian seminaries, Hebrew Bibles, prayerbooks, Haggadahs, manuscripts, rare early printed books that almost no one knew about. The books were all protected, even treasured in special vaults, but each one resided alone, scattered throughout the greater Philadelphia area. This was, I realized, a diaspora of Jewish books, and it became my project to gather them all together and, at least, for a short while, to make for them their own "homeland" in which they could reside together in their own space. After years of effort, I finally succeeded, and when I saw them all together I knew how Herzl would have felt had he lived to see the State of Israel.*

LOUIS KAHN: "OUR ARCHITECT"

Self-portrait by Louis Kahn. *Anne Tyng Foundation Collection.*

Louis I. Kahn has been called the greatest American architect since Frank Lloyd Wright. Sculptor Isamu Noguchi went further and called him a philosopher among architects.

Kahn's office was located in the City Center on the corner of Fifteenth and Walnut Streets. When not strolling the streets of his beloved city, he could be found teaching appreciative students at the University of Pennsylvania. Both Robert Venturi and Moshe Safdie apprenticed with him. Commissions took Kahn around the globe. But when asked why he did not set up shop in cutting-edge New York, Kahn answered, "Why would I want to be a Philadelphian living in New York City?" The trouble was that Kahn was more loyal to Philadelphia than the city was to him. For one thing, Philadelphia has always been conservative artistically. For another, Kahn was alienated from the Protestant elite who dominated the local architectural scene. As a result, Kahn's most notable achievements are not found in the City of Brotherly Love.

Born in Estonia in 1901, Kahn was taken by his family to Philadelphia in 1904, where he resided for the rest of his life. It is truly hard to imagine Kahn as a ladies' man. He was short and unattractive, and his face was badly scarred from a childhood accident. Yet he had simultaneous relationships with three women, maintained three households and had three children, all without each family's awareness of the others.

His love of architecture was inspired by a course in high school, and this led him to the University of Pennsylvania. Extremely poor, he managed to receive a complete scholarship. He studied with the famous city architect Paul Cret, who was the designer of the

Ben Franklin Parkway. Upon receiving a master's degree in 1924, he apprenticed with a firm in the city, eventually earning enough income to travel to Europe, including to his native Estonia, where he was enchanted by its medieval walled cities. He made drawings of ancient sites in Egypt and Greece. He responded to the monumental scale of ancient architecture and developed a preference for the natural materials of brick and stone over glass and steel. All of this would inform his style for a lifetime of building.

Kahn taught at Yale from 1947 to 1957. While there, he received his first significant commission: designing the Yale University Art Gallery (1951–53) and introducing innovative atmospheric controls that required no ducts. He later designed the Yale Center for British Art (1968–74).

When he was offered a professorship at the University of Pennsylvania's School of Design, he happily returned to Philadelphia and remained on the Penn faculty until his death in 1974. He married Esther Israeli, a research assistant. During rough financial periods, Esther's family would support them until his teaching flourished, and he received a commission to build the Richards Medical Building on campus between 1957 and 1962.

Kahn did not build many buildings. He knew what he wanted and would rather walk away from a commission than compromise himself. He was "the artist's artist," I.M. Pei stated in 2003 in an interview with Kahn's son, Nathaniel, in the Oscar-nominated documentary *My Architect*. Pei added that this obstinacy led Kahn to focus on quality rather than quantity. Kahn was destined to suffer great disappointments. Yet he was also to build some of the most memorable buildings of the twentieth century, including the following:

❖ *The Salk Institute in La Jolla, California (1959–67), dramatically perched on a cliff, with each lab office commanding a vista of the Pacific Ocean and including recessed natural lighting and a water element between the structures.*
❖ *The Kimberly Art Museum in Fort Worth, Texas (1967), featuring skylight ceilings that afforded all-natural, indirect lighting so as not to damage the art collection.*

❖ *The Capital Complex in Dhaka, Bangladesh (begun in 1962 but not completed until after Kahn's death). In Dhaka, Kahn had to overcome political unrest and harsh weather.*

❖ *The Indian Institute of Management in Ahmedabad, India (1962–74). These two buildings were the largest and most demanding work Kahn undertook.*

Two of the biggest disappointments in his life were the rejections of his plans for the Mikveh Israel Synagogue in Philadelphia and the Hurva (Ruin) Synagogue in the Jewish Quarter of the Old City of Jerusalem. Always a very spiritual man, though not religiously observant, Kahn would have been a brilliant choice for these projects. In both instances, he made concession after concession, eager to contribute to his own heritage. One can see drawings for both buildings at New York's Museum of Modern Art drawing library and at the University of Pennsylvania. How ironic that a Jew was to design his most spiritual structures for Muslim clientele in India and Pakistan, where his buildings are much revered.

Kahn's beloved Philadelphia nonetheless boasts three of his major designs. In addition to the Richards Medical Building on the Penn campus, we have two private residences in his mature style. These are the Fisher Home in suburban Hatboro and the Esherick Home in Chestnut Hill.

Kahn was a good friend of the frame maker turned carpenter turned master wood sculptor Wharton Esherick. This somewhat eccentric fellow lived like a hermit in a small home completely built by his own hands in Paoli, outside Philadelphia. Kahn would visit with him and talk art. Both had a deep respect for wood. Kahn was the obvious choice of Esherick's niece, Margaret, to design her home on a half-acre lot in Chestnut Hill, a ten-minute drive from Center City. It was commissioned in 1959 and completed in 1961. It received the Landmark Building Award from the American Institute of Architecture, Philadelphia Chapter, in 1992. The home was recently offered for sale in 2008 for $2–3 million but to date has remained unsold, due to its small size (it has only one bedroom). But Joe Rosa, curator of the Art Institute of Chicago, believes that this was Kahn's best residential structure.

Fisher Home interior by Louis Kahn. *Photograph by author.*

The Fisher Home was built after the Esherick Home and surely ranks as Kahn's most mature residential undertaking. Norman Fisher was a physician, and his wife, Doris, was a landscape designer. They commissioned Kahn to design their home in 1960. They had already purchased an attractive two-acre wooded lot in Hatboro, and Kahn seemed the obvious choice to build it for them. The doctor was also a skilled woodworker—we can see some of his sculpture and furniture in the home—and this made the men kindred spirits. The proximity of Pennypack Creek in the yard was another draw. Many of Kahn's spectacular buildings included an element of water in relationship to the structure. Discussions devoted to refining the design stretched over seven years. Said Norman Fisher, "Had we had known that, we might not have gone ahead." But then he added, "But we're glad we did." A scene in *My Architect* was filmed here with Kahn's son and daughters.

The Fisher Home, one of only three major private residences designed and realized by Kahn, will eventually be turned over to the National Trust for Historic Preservation. Fisher's daughters Claudia

The Norman Fisher Home. *Photograph by author.*

and Nina and their families still visit the home frequently. Both sisters animatedly told me that when they were kids they enjoyed hiding in the interesting cubby spaces and shimmying out of their ingenious bedroom windows into the yard. They said it was akin to living in a treehouse, particularly due to all the natural light and the home's openness.

One is immediately drawn to the core of the home, the huge fireplace. The stone was locally hewn in the spectrum of ores, grays and browns. Slightly whipping into the dining area, the shape is reminiscent of the enigmatic Iron Age brochs scattered throughout the Scottish Highlands. All monumental, all masonry, they were the precursors of castle towers used for defense against enemies and protection against storms. The understanding of these primal forms is the key to appreciating Kahn's artistry. This very turret motif was apparent in Kahn's sadly unrealized Mikveh Israel Synagogue.

The glass panels on the walls surrounding the fireplace look out at the garden, the creek and the sculptured bridge that Kahn also designed. Standing on the bridge, one can appreciate the grand, multi-angled view of the home. Do not, however, refer to it as the back of the home. Once, when Fisher was displeased with the placement of the utility meters by the entrance and requested that they be moved to the back of the home, Kahn replied, "There is no back to a home."

At the request of the homeowners, both for privacy and for reasons of security, I have not listed the addresses of the Esherick and Fisher Homes.

Kahn's earliest major commission was the Richards Medical Building on the University of Pennsylvania campus. With the understanding that the laboratories are the scientists' studios, Kahn created three stacks of work spaces attached to three tall service towers. The shapes are suggestive of a Tuscan hill town, such as the walled medieval San Gimignano. This represented a turning point in contemporary architecture, say Romaldo Giurgola and Jaimini Mehta in their book *Louis I. Kahn.*

The building was constructed between 1957 and 1961 and situated on Hamilton Walk between Thirty-seventh and Thirty-eighth Streets on the campus. Like expensive wine improved by age,

32

this gem established Kahn's reputation as a leading architect of the twentieth century. It was the first multistory, rigid-frame structure to employ pre-cast, pre-stressed and post-tensioned construction in the United States. The building was designated in January 2009 as a National Historic Landmark.

The Gershman Y: A Festive Place

The Gershman Y is located in the heart of Center City at 401 South Broad Street, just across the street from the new Kimmel Center for the Performing Arts (named for Sidney Kimmel, a major philanthropist to Jewish and other causes in Philadelphia). This stretch of Broad is known as the Avenue of the Arts and features the symphony hall, several theatres, a jazz club and a ballet company. The Y likewise offers a range of cultural and artistic activities. The Y grew out of Philadelphia's Young Men's Hebrew Association, which was founded in 1875 and, after adding a women's division, moved to its present location in 1926. With great numbers of Jews having moved from the city to the suburbs, the Gershman Y is no longer the central Jewish institution that it once was. Indeed, the building was recently sold to the neighboring University of the Arts. But the Y has a long-term lease from the university and has hardly abandoned its mission. In addition, the Y is home to Congregation Minyan Sulam Ya'akov, a lay-led congregation for unaffiliated city dwellers and for college students. There is also an auditorium for lectures and other events.

The Y is open daily from 9:00 a.m. to 5:00 p.m. For program information call 215-446-3021 or send an e-mail to events@gershmany.org.

The Gershman Y no longer offers a swimming pool or gymnasium, due to lack of funds for maintenance and modernization and due to the migration of Jews to newer gyms elsewhere in the city or to condos with pools and workout facilities.

The Y has also relinquished its cutting-edge status as a venue for modern art. Back in the 1960s, artists yet to be discovered in

The Kimmel Center's Verizon Hall, in African mahogany and shaped like a cello. *Photograph by Jim Roese. The Kimmel Center.*

The Kimmel Center for the Performing Arts, with its dramatic glass-vaulted ceiling, occupies an entire block on Broad Street between Fourteenth and Fifteenth Streets. The Kimmel, designed by Raphael Vinoly and completed in 2001, is home to the renowned Philadelphia Orchestra. *Photograph by Jeff Goldberg. The Kimmel Center.*

the New York art scene were shown at the Gershman's Borowsky Gallery. Veteran Y film festival chairperson Judy Golden tells of savvy women from Philly's YM&WHA Arts Council (as it was known then) heading off to New York in their fur coats to induce artists, as well as theatre and dance groups, to come to the Gershman. Allen Kaprow staged one of his first happenings in our city, and fellow Jewish artists Roy Lichtenstein, Christo and George Segal were welcomed at the Y. Other "discoveries" included Andy Warhol, Marisol Escobar and Claes Oldenburg. The wonderful local graphic artist Sam Maitin created striking posters to announce each event, including New York theatre productions, which arrived here on Mondays when the New York theatres were dark, and for companies like the Jose Limon Dance Company.

In April 2003, a brilliant retrospective of those creative years was held in the Gershman's Borowsky Gallery. It produced a catalogue called *A Happening Place*. The original participating artists' work graced our city once more. I spent hours in that exhibition, delighted by the art but saddened that, due to financial constraints, the Gershman is not the "happening" Philadelphia art venue it once was. Nevertheless, it still maintains the Borowsky Gallery for contemporary paintings and prints and the Open Lens Gallery for contemporary photographs, and these usually have very worthwhile exhibitions. The phone number for both galleries is 215-446-3001. Admission to both is free.

The Y also continues to offer a variety of programs, with book talks with visiting authors and with Hebrew literature classes, art, cooking, music appreciation, yoga and more. And not least, the Y sponsors three annual festivals that have become cherished Philadelphia traditions.

Latkepalooza celebrates Hanukkah. It serves up not your usual potato pancakes but rather latkes "interpreted" by some of the most noted restaurants in the city. Last season there were eleven choices. Asian fusion chef Joseph Poon of Joseph Poon Chef Kitchen in Chinatown put ginger and cilantro in latkes, Chief Fritz Blank of restaurant Deux Cheminees made an Alsace cabbage latke, chefs from Mediterranean restaurant Estia made spinach feta latkes and

The Foodbank. *Gershman Y.*

the Zahav restaurant featured a haute Israel-style concoction. Dare to try the sufganiot (fried jelly doughnuts) at the finish. Games, clowns and stories are all part of this event.

The Moo Shu Jew Show is a "Chinese Food on Christmas Day" event. Guests dine at a restaurant in nearby Chinatown, enjoying an eight-course meal and a stand-up comedy show, both on Christmas Eve and on Christmas Day. Each year, hundreds of Jewish Philadelphians make this their "Christmas tradition."

The Jewish Film Festival is held after the High Holidays and, after San Francisco's, is the second-oldest such festival in the country. The year 2010 marks its thirtieth season. The three-week event offers international features, independent films and documentaries, all concerning the Jewish experience. Distinguished filmmakers speak to film-loving audiences. In the spring, the Gershman Y also hosts a new filmmakers weekend.

In addition to the Gershman Y festivals, three more annual citywide Jewish events take place in Philadelphia.

Purim at the Zoo is celebrated at the Philadelphia Zoo, the nation's very first zoological garden. Designed in a Victorian style, terraced and stunningly landscaped, it's also one of the most beautiful zoos in the area. The zoo is host to an annual Purim party. Children in costumes gather for music, face painting, Purim arts and crafts and hamantashen. Activity booklets relating to the story of Purim are provided by the Auerbach Central Agency for Jewish Education. This event is sponsored by the *Jewish Exponent*, Philadelphia's venerable Jewish weekly, and began in 1993. Check the *Exponent* website (www.jewishexponent.com) for times and dates.

Holocaust Remembrance Day meets at the Holocaust Memorial at Sixteenth Street and the Ben Franklin Parkway (see the first section in part I). Holocaust survivors, their relatives and others gather at the *Monument to the Six Million Martyrs* sculpture on this day for prayer and meditation. This event was initiated by the Jewish community and is sponsored by the Jewish Community Relations Council, a constituent agency of the Jewish Federation of Greater Philadelphia.

Israel Independence Day is celebrated at the Eakins Oval opposite the Art Museum and the "Rocky" steps. This event is sponsored by the Jewish Federation of Greater Philadelphia. Attendance often reaches five thousand for a march of solidarity and support for the State of Israel. "Yom Ha'atzmaut" usually occurs in May and is scheduled "rain or shine," with participants requested to wear blue and white and to carry banners and Israeli flags. There are booths for Israeli arts and crafts, a Bedouin coffee tent and kosher food vendors. The stage in Eakins Oval features choirs and dance troupes. Participants often aim to make *The Guinness Book of World Records* for the world's largest hora circle

Israel Independence Day Parade on the Parkway. *Photograph by Scott H. Spitzer. Jewish Federation of Greater Philadelphia.*

by dancing around the oval. Parking on-site is almost impossible. Best to go by public transportation. Events begin near the SEPTA Regional Rail Suburban Station at Fifteenth and Market Streets. From the station, walk along the Franklin Parkway northwest from City Hall.

THE JEWISH RENAISSANCE
AT TEMPLE UNIVERSITY

"An explosion of Jewish study and culture leads to a veritable Jewish renaissance on the Temple campus," reports Aaron Passman in the September 10, 2009 issue of Philadelphia's *Jewish Exponent*. Like the University of Pennsylvania, Temple University also has a student population of about thirty thousand, and for a long time Temple was the first choice for Jewish Philadelphia students. Many were children of immigrants, often the first generation to enter college. As the city's only state-supported university, it was the affordable route. Over time, however, as other options came within reach, Temple's Jewish population diminished. Now with the recent recession and skyrocketing tuition at private colleges, Temple's Jewish population is growing again. Another favorable factor is that Temple is dramatically expanding its campus, adding more buildings and more programs—including some notable Jewish features. For the Jewish students this is a fortuitous moment in the 125-year-old Temple history. Jews at present make up approximately 10 percent of the student population.

Temple's Hillel organization recently moved from a tiny residence on Broad Street to a three-story brick and glass building, renamed the Edward H. Rosen Center, at Fifteenth and Norris Streets, with a rooftop terrace commanding a rare unobstructed view of the city. The building was dedicated on November 11, 2009, and it serves 80 percent of the Jewish undergrads living on campus. Hillel offers kosher food service, a TV lounge, a reading area, WiFi access and, importantly, social events, making it the campus hub for the three thousand Jewish students. In addition, the Rosen Center reaches out to the general campus population, welcoming all to its many programs and activities.

Temple's Feinstein Center of American Jewish History, founded by the late sociologist Murray Friedman, has a new director. Under Dr. Lila Corwin Berman, the center is providing resources for students and for the community at large, and for the first time it is offering public lectures, workshops, study grants and internships for researchers of American Jewish history.

The Edward H. Rosen Hillel Center for Jewish Life. *Hillel House.*

Temple's Jewish Studies Program meanwhile offers courses in Jewish culture, history, religion, philosophy, language and literature. Mark Leutcher heads this program and says that as far as he knows Temple is the only college in the country to offer certification in secular Judaism. Spinoza to Seinfeld is one of the many courses listed in the syllabus.

African Americans compose about 15 percent of Temple's student population, and the university interestingly has a new Center for Afro-Jewish Studies. This center was founded by Dr. Lewis Gordon, an African American Jew, who says the CAJS is "dedicated to scholarship based on an awareness of historical, religious, political and philosophical issues that arise from the convergence of the African and Jewish Diasporas." It is part of Temple's Institute for the Study of Race and Social Thought.

In another recent development, the Jewish Archive Center (JAC) merged with Temple's Urban Archives Center and is now located in the basement of Temple's Paley Library on the Temple Mall at Twelfth and Berks Streets. It was a difficult decision to close the original archive center, which was founded in 1972 as the historical repository of Philadelphia's Jewish Federation and American Jewish Committee. This archive was first housed in the basement of the Curtis Publishing Company, a space leased for one dollar per year. In 1985, the archive was moved to a now defunct facility called the Balch Institute. By 2005, more space was desperately needed, and new preservation methods were required. It was finally decided that the seventeenth- and eighteenth-century documents would go to the Historical Society of Pennsylvania and that the nineteenth- and twentieth-century documents would go to Temple's Urban Archives.

The JAC serves the Greater Philadelphia and southern New Jersey area. Archivist Sarah Sherman oversees twenty-five million documents, photographs and recorded stories. The archive is open to students and to the public and hosts researchers writing anything from scholarly papers to novels to documentary films. Its most frequent patrons are genealogists creating family trees. Another practical activity is researching proof of birth dates to receive Social Security benefits and proof for inheritance rights. Nonstudents must make appointments to visit, supply an anticipated list of materials to be researched and provide a photo ID to enter this secluded section of the Paley Library. The telephone number is 215-204-5750.

The JAC papers span nearly two hundred years of Philadelphia Jewish history. The new facilities at Temple provide the important climate-controlled conditions, with state-of-the-art preservation apparatus. Jonathan Sarna of Brandeis University, the dean of American Jewish historians, conducted research here and declared it one of the best Jewish archives in the nation.

The Feinstein Center's oral history collection contains taped and transcribed memoirs by Jews regarded as central to the development of the Philadelphia Jewish community.

Other oral histories from the Jewish Federation's archives include recordings of the entire population of Woodbine, New Jersey, a community established by Eastern European Jews in the early twentieth century. Another oral history was started in the 1970s, when women in the Federation jumped on the wave of the feminist movement to record history from a feminine point of view.

NOV 14 1917

letter No. 2. NATURALIZATION.

Date. *10/6/15*

Due. *10/6/17.*

Name. *Philip Applestein*

Address. *414 McClellan St*

Arrived at Port of

Application for 1st papers ✓

Application for 2nd papers

11/24/17 letter returned wrong address

From the Collections of the
PHILADELPHIA JEWISH ARCHIVES CENTER
TEMPLE UNIVERSITY LIBRARIES
URBAN ARCHIVES
1210 W. BERKS STREET
PHILADELPHIA, PA 19122

HIAS Naturalization Cards Prior to 1940, Aaron–Berland (ov) 367

HIAS house naturalization card prior to 1940. *Philadelphia Jewish Archives Center, Temple University Urban Archives.*

Records of immigrants arriving at the port of Philadelphia since 1884 were compiled by the Hebrew Immigrant Aid Society. The documents show that HIAS helped immigrants in negotiating the citizenship process and in finding relatives, housing, jobs and language lessons. HIAS also helped immigrants open bank accounts and noted that these banks served as "travel agents," places at which individuals saved money to bring over family members from Europe. As archivist Sarah Sherman began showing me one of the larger bank logs, I was inspired to ask her to try to find my husband's family, who entered the United States via the port of Philadelphia in the early 1900s. Sure enough, we found that Bubbie Esther Nesvisky (who handled the family finances) had made a bank deposit toward a steamship ticket purchase to bring over a cousin in 1902. Listed as well were the ship's name, the arrival date and even the Philadelphia street name and house number where the family lived.

Sarah Sherman says that the JAC's bank ledgers are the most robust collection of their type in the country. New York has none, she says, and Baltimore and Boston have only a few. She believes that more ledgers are still out there waiting to be found, and she hopes that they will find their way to join the wonderful resources in this new and modern home.

THREE ARCHIVES: ON THE RECORD

Even if you are not normally excited by collections of books, the three libraries and archives discussed here just might set your pulse racing, especially if you're doing Jewish genealogy, researching other Jewish topics or simply appreciating objects of antiquity and beauty.

The Historical Society of Pennsylvania

Founded in 1824 in Philadelphia, the Historical Society of Pennsylvania (HSP) is one of the oldest historical associations in America, housing some 600,000 printed items and over 19 million manuscript and graphic items. It has just celebrated its 100th anniversary in its present location, having moved to this totally fireproofed building in 1910.

The society is one of the largest genealogical libraries in the nation, with documents from the seventeenth through the

Historical Society of Pennsylvania. *Photograph by author.*

nineteenth centuries. Holdings were expanded with the addition of the collections of the Balch Institute for Ethnic Studies in 2002 and the Genealogical Society of Pennsylvania in 2006. These helped to make the Historical Society of Pennsylvania a major center for the documentation and study of ethnic communities and immigrant experiences. Since 2009, the HSP archives have been administered by the Atwater Kent Museum of Philadelphia.

Today the archives include a wide-ranging Jewish Genealogical collection, reports Senior Director Lee Arnold. He presented me with an eight-page Jewish research booklet, which is available at the desk. The booklet lists hundreds of resources, categorized by genealogies, synagogues, cemeteries, periodicals, photographs and image listings. The library is non-circulating, and the stacks are closed, but staff will walk the novice through the complex system. Lee Arnold notes that the library's small entrance fee entitles visitors to use the JewishGen genealogy website and is thus more economical than using the site's own website. Arnold also says the HSP has a large collection of Gratz memorabilia, autographed books from the Gratz library and Gratz correspondence with luminaries including Galileo and several popes.

The historical society is located at 1300 Locust Street, one block east of the Avenue of the Arts (Broad Street). In 1966, it sold the property next door to the venerable Library Company of Philadelphia. Both research institutions conveniently share resources and even have a secret door to connect them, reveals Arnold. The Library Company, after all, was originally established by none other than Benjamin Franklin in 1731. A marble sculpture of Franklin wearing a toga (!) was moved into the newer location and can be viewed through the large glass window. The HSP building itself is listed on Philadelphia's Register of Historical Places.

HSP Library hours: Tuesday and Thursday, 12:30 p.m. to 5:30 p.m.; Wednesday, 12:30 p.m. to 8:30 p.m.; and Friday, 10:00 a.m. to 5:30 p.m. See the website at www.hsp.org.

The Library Company of Philadelphia

The Library Company was an offshoot of Ben Franklin's Junto, an intellectual and political discussion group. Books were expensive commodities in colonial Philadelphian, so Franklin intuited that by assembling a group of investors many books could be purchased and shared. He commissioned bibliophile James Logan to sail to London for the initial purchases. Thus, the oldest subscription library in the country was established. It remains the oldest intact colonial library to this day and is still a privately run lending and research library (borrowers pay deposits on items they take home).

Logan was the appropriate choice for this task. This prominent Quaker owned one of the largest book collections of his day and, incidentally, the largest collection of Jewish and Hebrew books in the colonies. He had accompanied William Penn from England in 1699 to be Penn's colony administrator. In 1722, Logan was chosen the first mayor of Philadelphia. So large was Logan's collection of books that when he died it became the core of the Library Company.

The establishment of the city's vast Free Library on the Parkway in 1927 meant the overshadowing of the private Library Company as a lending library and research institution. Noted book scholar Edwin Wolf II (coauthor of a popular book called *The History of the Jews of Philadelphia*) was hired in 1953 to make recommendations toward clarifying the purpose of the Library Company.

The library was so pleased with Wolf's ideas that he was immediately hired as librarian/curator, a position he held until he retired in 1984. Wolf gave his own collection to the Library Company in 1989, two years before his death. Over the course of his remarkable thirty-two-year directorship, Wolf was credited with reviving the library and giving it new purpose. One of his first moves was to create the Loganian Library room immediately to the right of the entrance. The room, with its long, dark, mahogany bookcase, conference table, oil paintings and marble busts of colonial dignitaries (no Greeks or Romans here!), is filled with

Bookcase in the Logan Room at the Library Company. *Photograph by author.*

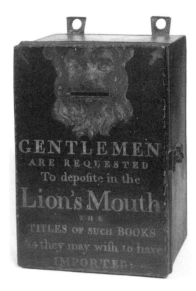

The Ben Franklin suggestion box in the Library Company. *The Library Company of Philadelphia.*

handsome antiquarian volumes, most of which had been imported from England by colonial Americans. Logan's personal library was a gentleman scholar's library; Wolf supplemented this with popular reading material of the colonial period, which are displayed in the Logan Room. A charming touch is Ben Franklin's suggestion box, in which the original library subscribers suggested book titles, dropping their requests through the slot of the lion's mouth.

The Library Company has approximately 500,000 books, periodicals, broadsides and other printed items. For our Jewish readers, Logan's Hebraic collection makes this a "must see" destination. The Print Department has approximately 75,000 items, primarily prints, photographs and maps. It also has first editions of both *Moby Dick* and *Leaves of Grass*. The Library Company is open Monday through Friday, 9:00 a.m. to 4:45 p.m. Its website is www.librarycompany.org or call 215-546-318.

Philadelphia Free Library

"Archives are like infrastructure—nobody wants to fund infrastructure," says Jonathan Sarna, professor of American Jewish history at Brandeis University. "On one hand, everybody wants to see records preserved. On the other hand, they're not really a funding priority for anybody." Marion Parkinson, assistant librarian in the Philadelphia Free Library's Education, Philosophy and Religion (EPR) Department, knows this quite well. In 2002, the city's central library received a $2.5 million annual budget. Today it receives

Philadelphia Free Library on the Ben Franklin Parkway. *Photograph by author.*

$550,000. According to the Public Library Survey, Pennsylvania in fact ranks thirty-ninth in state spending for libraries. Pennsylvania also has one of the lowest rates of library visits per person, while neighboring Ohio has the highest.

When I asked Marion about the number of people using the archives in her department, she sadly answered, "Almost none." This is a shame, not least because the terribly underfunded library's archives contain some unique Jewish resources. Among these resources is the Moses Marx Collection. This private library consists of over three thousand volumes purchased by the Free Library in 1927 with money from the Simon Gratz Fund. Gratz had been on the library's board of trustees when he initiated this fund. Moses Marx, himself a librarian and publisher of Jewish books in Germany, had created a comprehensive library of Hebrew printing in fifteenth- and sixteenth-century Germany. Only about half of his collection has been catalogued and preserved in the vault of the EPR department. The remainder waits to be catalogued by

Amity Doering, a former head of the EPR who now works on the project on a volunteer basis, filing, binding and boxing the books and manuscripts in acid-free containers. Locking the vault, Marion Parkinson next took me to view the stacks.

One picture is worth a thousand words, and that is why we have a photograph from one section of the six floors of the closed stacks. Regarding the Jewish books to be found in the EPR Department, Marion Parkinson explained how to search the collection on the Internet: go to www.freelibrary.org and click on "catalogue" and then the term "Jewish" and you get 6,286 results. Then click on the various formats and subjects to get an idea of what is held in each department of the Free Library. In the subject list, 2,124 items come up under Jews, 1,087 for the Holocaust, 600 for Judaism and so on.

My last stop in this city block–sized library was the Rare Books Department on the third floor, accessible only with a staff person and by a special elevator. (Visiting this sequestered archive, I felt like I was in a Dan Brown novel.) This department has one of the

Closed stacks at the Philadelphia Free Library. *Photograph by author.*

Left: *Balance Sheet of Extermination* pamphlet cover, an American Jewish Congress publication from 1945 recently found in the stacks of the Philadelphia Free Library. *Photograph by author.*

Below: The popular computer room in the Free Library. *Photograph by author.*

largest rare book collections of any public library in the United States. Scholars and school students may visit. Art students with an interest in calligraphy come to see manuscripts in Hebrew, Persian, Armenian, Arabic and other nonwestern script—even cuneiform. Many manuscripts in the Hebraic collection are from the medieval Italian era. Head Archivist of the Rare Book Department Janine Pollack put on white cotton gloves and placed a 1496 Masoretic Bible from Lisbon, printed on vellum and leather-bound, onto the bookstand in front of me. The Bible was decorated in the Damascus style, with carpet border motifs and liberal amounts of gold leaf and lavish color. This is one of the most highly treasured Hebraic books in the collection. We also examined two Esther scrolls in long glass cases.

Yet another resource is located in the Print and Picture Collection Department. A substantial folder labeled "Jewish" has hundreds of images of Jewish holidays, ritual objects and manuscript images to borrow, photograph and use for publication purposes. This is another handy resource for artists, writers and historians.

Who knew that Philadelphia's public library was such a treasure house of Judaica?

The Philadelphia Free Library is located at 1901 Vine Street between Nineteenth and Twentieth Streets on the Benjamin Franklin Parkway. Open Monday through Thursday, 9:00 a.m. to 9:00 p.m.; Friday, 9:00 a.m. to 6:00 p.m.; and Saturday, 9:00 a.m.to 5:00 p.m. Call at 215-686-5322.

UPenn's Museum:
Old Wine in Old Bottles

The Museum of Archaeology and Anthropology, located at 3260 South Street on the campus of the University of Pennsylvania, houses exhibits from all over the world, with especially valuable Egyptian, Near Eastern and Far Eastern Collections. Founded in 1887, the museum has sponsored over four hundred expeditions all over the world to explore humanity's collective heritage. The

Pond outside the main entrance of the Museum of Archaeology and Anthropology University of Pennsylvania. *Museum of Archaeology and Anthropology University of Pennsylvania.*

building is designed in the classic Beaux Arts style and is one of the most notable of Penn campus landmarks. (My grandchildren, who are very much into wizardly lore, especially like the crystal ball located in the Chinese Rotunda.) One could spend hours exploring all three floors of the museum, but we will focus on finds concerning Jewish heritage.

Of particular Jewish interest are two exhibits in galleries opposite each other on the second floor. To the right of the second-floor landing, enter the first hall for the Iraq exhibit, which dates back six millennia. After this, head across the hall to the Israel/Canaanite exhibits. (To archaeologists, Canaan is more than the biblical Land of Israel; it includes portions of today's southern Syria and Lebanon.)

Pam Kosty, assistant director for Public Information, led me through the Iraq exhibition, probably the most famous collection in the museum. The entrance wall text states: "Your origin and your birth are from the land of the Canaanite" (Ezekiel 16:3). I learned that the University of Pennsylvania archaeologists were part of a team that included counterparts from Iraq and from the British

Museum. Led by the renowned Leonard Woolley in 1922, the team's excavations revealed the remains of Sumerian culture at its zenith in the city of Ur, in southern Iraq. In the Book of Genesis, Abraham sets out from Ur toward the promised land. Tel el-Mukayyan is the present name of this site. This ancient Mesopotamian settlement is more than 4,500 years old, and as such, its artifacts are the most valued of the museum's rich collections.

Those excavations in 1922 caused a sensation in the world press, and the uncovering of Ur's royal tombs inspired Agatha

Ram Caught in a Thicket from the Iraq exhibit at the Museum of Archaeology and Anthropology University of Pennsylvania. *Museum of Archaeology and Anthropology University of Pennsylvania.*

Christie to travel there to research the setting of her novel *Murder in Mesopotamia*. (She eventually married Woolley's assistant.) The greatest find was that of Queen Pu-Abi's tomb, amazingly untouched by looters. Her skeleton was preserved along with that of two others, probably her attendants to serve her in her afterworld. Woolley believed that they drank poison and died peacefully. Attempting to confirm Woolley's theory, the servants' skulls were taken to UPenn's Hospital to be CAT-scanned (very early in the morning, reports Pam Kosty, so as not to freak out the patients). The researchers discovered that the deaths were caused by blows to the skull.

Other outstanding pieces in the collection are a bull-headed lyre representing Shamash, the sun god. It's a 27-inch-tall musical instrument typically played at banquets and made of gold, silver and lapis. Also notable is the 16.5-inch-high free-standing sculpture called *Ram Caught in a Thicket*, made of gold, lapis, copper, shell, red limestone and bitumen. One half of Woolley's finds remained in Iraq, and the remaining items were equally divided between Penn and the British museum. All told, over one million objects were divided up. UPenn is certainly lucky to have acquired these items.

Leaving the Iraq exhibition, I crossed the hall to meet Patrick McGovern. He is adjunct professor of anthropology, and among his numerous roles is scientific director of the Biomolecular Archaeology Laboratory. As in the example of the CAT scan employed to examine the skulls in Queen Pu-Abi's tomb, much of archaeology is being reinterpreted today thanks to modern technology and particularly through DNA studies. Interpreting ancient wines and understanding ancient dye processes are two of Professor McGovern's special interests. He guided me to two display cases holding items found in the Baq'ah Valley, nine miles northwest of Amman, Jordan, a site where he worked between 1977 and 1981. After leaving the Iraq exhibit of finds 4,500 years old, this qualified as the modern period, fully two millennia more recent. Yet the stacking bowl wine set made me think of modern times.

These bowls are sized according to one's thirst, with a juglet and strainer to filter the wine nestled into the smallest bowl. What a wonderful wedding gift—only this wine set is from the Late Bronze Age between 1300 and 1200 BCE, so presumably it's rather pricey.

Wine set from the Ancient Israel exhibit at the Museum of Archaeology and Anthropology University of Pennsylvania. *Museum of Archaeology and Anthropology University of Pennsylvania.*

Professor McGovern likes to point out that wine is mentioned over 140 times in the Bible. (Beer is not mentioned once.) He noted that wine was a major source of energy; 10 percent of our livers, he said, are composed of enzymes that convert alcohol into energy. I also learned that clay amphorae (wine jugs) dating as far back as five thousand years had been found in tombs, palaces and temples and that the vessels were often stamped to indicate quality (good, very good or very, very good). Shown as well is the date when the wine was produced and even the names of the vintner and the region where the wine was produced. Shiraz, one of my favorites, was made in the vicinity of Persia in 3000–2500 BCE. To celebrate McGovern's latest book, *Uncorking the Past: The Quest for Wine, Beer, and Other Alcoholic Beverages* (University of California Press), an evening of wine tasting and scholarly talk was held at the museum in October 2009.

In the next case over, the professor showed me a collection of Phoenician juglets with purple dye stains. These vessels were found all along the Mediterranean port of Sarepta, where a dye factory existed during the same period the wine set was made. Ten thousand *Murex trunculus* mollusk shells were needed to produce one gram of this dye, so precious that only the high priests of ancient Israel could wear the garments colored with it. In the Bible, this color is called argamon, as mentioned in Exodus 25:8, which gives details of the priestly garments. The dye is also mentioned by name in the Talmud. Sherds of the mollusk shells from the coastal area between Acre and Tyre were also found on Jerusalem's Temple Mount dating from the First Temple period. By the Second Temple period, all evidence of this mollusk was gone. In describing the priestly color, kabbalists state that the word argamon is derived from the initials of five angels mentioned in the Bible and in the Talmud: Uriel (spelled with an *aleph* in Hebrew), Raphael, Gabriel, Michael and Nuriel. Argamon is actually a combination of colors derived from these mollusk shells. Indigo is called "techelet" in Hebrew and, in addition to the cloth used to make the priestly garments, was also used to dye one of the strands of the fringe of the prayer shawl to be worn by all males.

Techelet was meant to connect the one who prays to the Temple. Apparently this mollusk was also found in the Sea of Galilee, suggesting that it somehow migrated (or was carried) from the sea onto the land and thence to the freshwater lake. The techelet dye, no longer extant, was never replaced by any other natural or synthetic dye. Thus there is no longer a blue strand in the prayer shawl.

This exhibition also includes artifacts excavated from the Bet She'an catacombs in Israel. All told, the exhibition has more than 350 rare artifacts dating from 3000 to 500 BCE. Most of the objects were found in Israel, Jordan and Lebanon.

The University of Pennsylvania Museum of Archaeology and Anthropology is conveniently located right by the Regional Rail's University City station. Take R1, R2 or R3 trains setting out from the Market East station at Market and Twelfth Streets in City Center. Exit at the University City station to the street, walk a few yards forward and turn right into the Kress entrance of the museum. However, to really appreciate the exterior beauty of the museum, one should turn to the right from the University City exit, walk to the corner, cross the street and head left on South Street toward the main entrance, opposite the fish pond. The museum is open Tuesday through Saturday 10:00 a.m. to 4:30 p.m. and Sundays 1:00 to 5:00 p.m. Admission is ten dollars for adults and seven dollars for seniors and for youths aged six through seventeen. Check out its website at www.penn.museum for program details or call 215-898-4000. The museum offers guided tours, audio tours, a café and two craft stores.

In addition to the museum, UPenn offers an undergraduate major in Jewish Studies, as well as graduate training in the field through various Penn departments. The Jewish Studies Program has courses in history, religion, literature, languages, texts, politics and culture. Professor Beth Wenger is the program director. In addition to the interdisciplinary major in Jewish Studies, there are also concentrations in Jewish history in the History Department, in Jewish texts in the Department of Near Eastern Language and Civilizations and in Judaism in the Department of Religious Studies. Penn's Herbert D. Katz Center for Advanced Judaic Studies focuses on postdoctoral research, and the Penn libraries contain one of the world's foremost Judaica collections.

Penn also has an excellent Jewish community outreach program. Christine Walsh is administrative coordinator of the Jewish Studies Program. Persons signing up for the mailing list at jsp-info@sas.upenn. edu receive announcements about lectures, films, book talks, concerts and even dinners. These programs are free and open to the public.

CONGREGATION RODEPH SHALOM: MOORISH AND MODERN

This monumental synagogue is undoubtedly one of the most beautiful in our city and is well worth a visit for its architecture, history and museums. It's located at 615 North Broad Street, between Green and Vernon Streets, five blocks from City Hall. Its architecture is Moorish Revival, and it was designed in 1870 by Frank Furness, a leading architect of the time. Furness built on a grandiose scale, had a strong sense of the decorative and designed many outstanding buildings in Philadelphia during the Victorian era, the most economically robust period in the city's history. Another example of his lavish work is the Pennsylvania Academy of Fine Art located on North Broad at Cherry Street, built between 1872 and 1876. There the rich brick patterns in Venetian red and ivory, and the interior ceiling in cerulean blue and gold-leaf floral patterns, make for an eclectic and grandiose building, combining English, Italian and French motifs.

Rodeph Shalom and the Academy of Fine Art are among Furness's finest buildings to be completed for the 1876 American Centennial celebration held in Philadelphia. The Academy was the first museum and art school in the nation, while the synagogue was one of the earliest Reform congregations in the nation.

Moorish Revival was a typical synagogue style in the late 1800s and early 1900s, first in Europe and then in America. The style both reflected the Romantic fascination with all things oriental and recalled the Golden Age of Jewry in medieval Spain. Moorish Revival was the antithesis of the Gothic style, with domes and rounded forms replacing spires and with Ottoman-style motifs replacing the somber Gothic interiors. Moorish Revival also featured lavish patterns in vaulted mosaic ceilings and carpeted floors in an array of colors. The Rodeph Shalom sanctuary is especially noted for its large pendentive dome, and the magnificent Ark has intricately carved doors flanked by marble columns.

Another reason why a Moorish style was favored for a massive synagogue was the avoidance of any resemblance to a cathedral. Traditionally, cathedrals had been associated with anti-Semitism, with their sculpture, paintings and caryatids frequently portraying negative images of the Jewish people. A standard feature of medieval German cathedrals, for example, was statuary portraying Jews wearing pointed hats and suckling from a sow. In France, opposite entrance portals of Cathedral Notre Dame, the persona sculpture *Ecclesia* (The Church) contrasts with the persona sculpture *Synagoga*. Ecclesia is youthful, stands upright and has a halo and staff. Synagoga is hunched over, significantly older, blinded by the crown fallen over her eyes and has a snake around her head. The church's message was to depict the blindness of the Jews to the truth of Christianity.

Congregation Rodeph Shalom. *Photograph by Graydon Wood, courtesy Martin Jay Rosenblum, American Institute of Architects.*

The sanctuary of Congregation Rodeph Shalom. *Photograph by Graydon Wood, courtesy Martin Jay Rosenblum, American Institute of Architects.*

Among the finest examples of Moorish Revival synagogues in the United States are Manhattan's Park East Synagogue, Cincinnati's Plum Street Synagogue and our own Rodeph Shalom, which in fact was greatly inspired by the main synagogue in Florence, Italy.

Rodeph Shalom was founded in 1795 and claims on its website to be the oldest Ashkenazi synagogue in the Western Hemisphere. With the lone and perhaps obvious exception of Beth Sholom, which we will discuss next, Philadelphians customarily refer to their synagogues by their initials. Thus, Rodeph Shalom is popularly known as RS.

The founding members of RS left the Mikveh Israel Synagogue, which at the time was the sole synagogue in Philadelphia. The breakaway faction preferred to form a congregation based on its own Ashkenazic minhagim (traditions) and not Sephardic ones. While Sephardim and Askenazim read from the same prayer book, their melodies are markedly different, as are their synagogue layouts. In Sephardic custom, the rabbi's pulpit is placed somewhere in the back of the sanctuary, with the rabbi facing the Ark of the Torah. In Ashkenazic tradition, the rabbi's pulpit is forward in the sanctuary, with the rabbi's back to the Ark.

These are not overwhelming differences, but couple them with a language barrier. The established MI congregation had assimilated and included English in its prayer, sermons, constitution and even note-taking during administrative meetings. The Ashkenazic newcomers were accustomed to speaking Yiddish among themselves and even with their non-Jewish neighbors back in Eastern Europe. In addition, the Ashkenazim were considerably poorer than the well-established Sephardic members of MI. So it was a religious, cultural and economic divide that led the newcomers to leave and form their own congregation, which they named the German Hebrew Congregation Rodeph Shalom. Their first edifice was dedicated in 1802. Their archives and notes were kept in Yiddish, and it is a real tragedy that many of these papers were destroyed by fire in 1839. As a result, very little of the early personal history of the congregation is known.

Both congregations, of course, were Orthodox—the only branch of Judaism at the time—and women and men sat in their own sections. It was not until 1901 that RS broke completely with Orthodoxy and embraced the Reform ideals emerging from Germany and being introduced to the United States. RS indeed was the pathfinder in Philadelphia and in our nation in regard to the establishment of Reform Judaism.

There are two museums located within the synagogue: the Philadelphia Museum of Jewish Art, founded in 1975 for contemporary exhibitions by Jewish artists and housing a permanent collection of modern arts and crafts, and the Obermayer Collection of Judaic Ritual Objects, which features traditional finials, spice and tzedakah boxes, menorahs, scrolls and the like.

The Museum of Jewish Art and the Obermayer are open Monday through Thursday, 10:00 a.m. to 4:00 p.m., and Friday, 10:00 a.m. to 2:00 p.m., although these hours tend to vary. Best to check in advance by calling 215-627-6747.

As more and more Jews began moving to the suburbs, RS established a second building in Elkins Park in the late 1950s. Then attrition, functional logistics and the return to the city of adults after child-raising caused the second synagogue to close. It was taken over by newly established Kol Ami, another Reform institution led by Rabbi Elliot Holin—a former associate rabbi of RS in the city. William I. Kuhn is currently rabbi for the 1,100 RS family members. Beth Ahava, the Delaware Valley's only gay and lesbian synagogue, recently became affiliated with RS and now meets there as well. Its members have dual congregational memberships.

RS, in a joint project with Federation Early Learning Services (FELS), recently purchased property across the street for an early learning center serving as a community outreach institution. Along those lines, with confirmation enrollment increasing, the next generation begins in the new building.

BETH SHOLOM'S JUBILEE YEAR

My first impression when driving past the Conservative congregation Beth Sholom Synagogue situated at the crest of Old

York Road was that aliens had landed in Elkins Park. I saw a huge, ornate, tent-shaped aluminum and glass structure aglow in the night sky. Set off from the highway, it appeared to be hovering. I almost drove off the road. I suppose viewing the hexagonal structure from the air, easy to spot on a dark night, could indeed attract aliens thinking it was the mother ship. Once inside, I found the interior somewhat shamanistic, with the huge multihued Eternal Light shaped like a rocket appearing as if it were about to take off, its "fuselage" bulbs capable of flashing code.

Indeed, I found it hard to believe that Frank Lloyd Wright had designed it. I once saw a wooden model of this Beth Sholom in the collection of historic model synagogues in the Museum of the Diaspora at Tel Aviv University. There were eighteen miniature synagogues exhibited, each from a different period. Beth Sholom's edifice represented the twentieth century as the prototype of a modern synagogue. Seeing it in miniature was one thing. Seeing it full-sized was something else.

The architect died four months before its dedication on September 20, 1959. He was ninety-two years old. The synagogue was among his last projects. Both Beth Sholom's Rabbi Mortimer Cohen and the architect were visionaries possessing strong ideas about the concept and design of the building. The rabbi wanted a modern "American" structure celebrating the 300th year of Jewish presence in America. Wright was likewise not content to build a synagogue in a traditional style but wanted rather a modern religious institution for American Jews. So there was a meeting of the minds at least concerning this idea. Yet their negotiations went on for six years, with the rabbi all the time explaining the iconography and ritual objects needed for a synagogue. In 1954, Wright presented his drawings to Rabbi Cohen. The architect wrote, "Herewith the promised 'hosanna'—a temple that is truly a religious tribute to a living God." To which Cohen replied, "You have taken the supreme moment of Jewish history—the revelation of God to Israel through Moses at Mount Sinai…You built Mount Sinai."

Cohen's Beth Sholom was originally established in the Logan area of Philadelphia in 1919. He began officiating there immediately after his ordination from New York's Jewish Theological Seminary that same year. He would later receive his PhD in Hebrew and cognate studies from Dropsie College in Philadelphia in 1935. In the early 1950s, Cohen witnessed the exodus of the Jewish population to the suburbs and felt that his synagogue had to follow suit. His decision would make Beth Sholom the first Philadelphia congregation to undertake such a move. Not wishing for the traditional Moorish or Gothic structure, but rather a uniquely twentieth-century Jewish house of worship, Cohen turned to his friend Boris Blai, the dean of Philadelphia's prestigious Tyler Art School, who proposed his friend Frank Lloyd Wright for the job.

Congregants opposed both the move and the notion of a modern building, as well as the choice of Frank Lloyd Wright—so avant-garde for the time and so expensive. So Cohen took the bold step and invited the architect to come to a lavish dinner at the Warwick Hotel, in the heart of City Center, to meet with the synagogue's board. And so it was that the world's most renowned architect convinced them to go ahead. Wright was given a retainer to start designing even before anyone knew the final cost or where the money would come from. Six years later, the building was completed. It was different from any building Wright had previously undertaken. A version of his design, however, had originally been conceived as a cathedral in 1920s but was then rejected and placed on the back burner by the master builder. Among the cathedral's startling features were the three steel beams serving as a towering canopy for the sanctuary. That concept would carry over. Wright justifiably wished to do something with this idea before he died. The three-ribbed frame was the base for the grand tentlike roof of Beth Sholom. That unusual shape must have been great fun to watch being built.

Interestingly, this was Wright's sole building for which he credited two people—himself and Rabbi Cohen—in its design. Nine volumes lining a shelf on Beth Sholom executive director Harvey Friedrich's bookcase attest to this collaboration. Cohen himself presented drawings based on those in the Book of Exodus dealing with the building of the Tabernacle. (See Exodus chapters 25–27 and chapters 35–38 and First Kings 5:26–6:13.) Wright in turn based his construction on the rabbi's renderings. In other words, with Rabbi Cohen's guidance, the ancient descriptions in

Beth Sholom Synagogue. *Congregation Beth Sholom.*

the Bible, along with the rabbi's interpretations, were incorporated into Wright's blueprints.

The three steel columns created a hexagonal exterior motif and are repeated inside. The cupped-hand shape is meant to symbolize hands in priestly blessing beckoning the congregation. And although the sanctuary seats 1,130, it feels intimate. The seats are arranged in a semicircle around the bimah. Congregants say that this arrangement makes them feel more like participants than an audience, and some members have told me that the space makes them feel like they are resting in the hands of God. The floor gently drops and is uniquely graded, allowing for unobstructed views of the pulpit. The lower pulpit concept allows for "teaching" and not "preaching."

The pulpit has two tall menorahs designed by Wright, and the Ark contains ten scrolls representing the Ten Commandments. Emblazoned above the Ark is the word *Kadosh* ("holy") melded with three medals symbolizing the passage in Isaiah 6:3: "Holy, holy, holy is the Lord of hosts: the whole earth is full of his glory." Pale beige carpeting and earth tone seats create an austere environment. The only interior color comes from the massive Eternal Light, which drops twenty-seven feet from the ceiling, and the raised Holy Ark. Wright's hexagonal cupped-hand motif appears everywhere, from the light switch plates to interior cabinets to the exterior pool on the grounds opposite the entrance.

The cost of construction was $1.4 million, three times more than the original estimate. Wright was never concerned about the money somehow appearing, though Rabbi Cohen spent many restless nights worrying about it.

When the building was completed in 1959, Dwight Eisenhower sent a letter of congratulations from the White House. Today the synagogue is listed on the National Register of Historic Landmarks. The National Trust for Historic Preservation has called it an invaluable contribution to American culture. The critic Brendan Gill said that the design was one of the most important during Wright's lifetime.

This was a dazzling sight to behold. Wright generally liked to integrate his buildings into the environment. However, when the occasion arose, he felt that some buildings should stand apart, like his bold Solomon R. Guggenheim Museum in New York. Author Susan Solomon, in *Louis I. Kahn's Jewish Architecture*, likens Beth Sholom to a religious skyscraper. The dramatic dome stands 110 feet high, the equivalent of an eleven-story building. Wright usually built with organic materials, but this synagogue is made of glass and aluminum. And yes, maintenance is costly. The tent-shaped roof leaked. Once the congregation got drenched, and all the carpeting had to be replaced. Parts of the roof blew away. A recent grant of $75,000 from the J. Paul Getty Foundation will help the congregation maintain this unique house of worship.

The synagogue celebrated its Jubilee Year on November 15, 2009, by inaugurating a Visitors Center within the building. James Kolker, the center's designer, recalled celebrating his bar mitzvah at Beth Sholom many years before and noted that the building has remained unchanged since then. At the inauguration, New York architecture critic Paul Goldberger opined that the building transcends time and is a truly sacred space. He also observed that Beth Sholom was built before the Kennedy era and that by presaging the jet age it

Holy Ark/Ner Tamid (Eternal Light) at Beth Sholom Synagogue in Elkins Park. *Congregation Beth Sholom.*

"both expressed the great American spirit and was an inspiration for generations to come."

Before the Visitors Center opened, the synagogue drew about 3,500 visitors annually. With the new facility, the synagogue expects that number to double. The center makes it possible for walk-ins to receive guided tours of the synagogue. One can now purchase a ticket, see an excellent twenty-minute documentary about the building narrated by actor Leonard Nimoy, view selections of archival material from Rabbi Cohen and Frank Lloyd Wright, see the architect's renderings and observe the timeline of the structure. Another attraction is the design store. The entrance to the Visitors Center is easily accessible via the parking lot at the Foxcroft Road entrance, near the corner of Old York Road. It is open Wednesday and Thursday between 10:00 a.m. and 1:00 p.m., and Sunday 10:00 a.m. to 3:00 p.m. Special arrangements can be made for groups. Emily Cooperman heads the newly created Beth Sholom Preservation Foundation, an independent nonprofit entity that oversees the Visitors Center (contact at 215-887-1342 or www. bethsholompreservation.org).

Now let's talk about the congregation itself. Remarkably, Beth Sholom has had only three major rabbinic eras since 1919. Rabbi Aaron Landes replaced Rabbi Mortimer Cohen in 1964. Landes came from a prestigious family of rabbis and was a chaplain and an admiral in the U.S. Naval Reserves. His term ended in 2004, and he is now the rabbi emeritus. At present, the congregation is led by Rabbi David Glanzberg-Krainin. Minyans are held twice daily, with 40 to 60 in attendance. It has about 950 family members, dramatically down from its peak membership of 1,300 in the 1960s.

In a recent interview, "Rabbi G-K," as he is often called, said that just walking into his extraordinary sanctuary quiets him and sets the tone for the service. Regarding the declining membership of Beth Sholom (and of many other neighboring congregations), the rabbi expressed the hope that education will be the key for growth and proudly mentioned recently receiving a $30,000 Legacy Heritage Education Grant, funded by the Legacy Heritage Fund in New York. Only twenty synagogues throughout the world have received this grant, and Beth Sholom is the only one in the region to receive it. The new funds allow for development of the synagogue's Montessori classes, its developmental track preschool programs, its after-school programs and experimental programs for its youth and adult education groups. The goal, says the rabbi, is to create a community committed to remaining in Elkins Park and to Judaism.

Rabbi G-K also boasts of the Junior Torah Reader's Club, where 90 percent of the congregation's post–bar mitzvah and post–bat mitzvah youth continue honing their Hebrew skills and Torah knowledge. Beth Sholom offers a special incentive: a guardian angel from the congregation greases the kids' palms with eighteen dollars each time they come to read the Torah. If they come weekly, the kids can do pretty well.

Whatever works.

KENESETH ISRAEL'S REMARKABLE RABBIS

Keneseth Israel was Philadelphia's preeminent Reform congregation almost from its inception. In March 1847, KI was established on Broad Street as the city's fourth Orthodox synagogue. After a short time, however, it aligned with the newly emerging Reform Movement and remained the only Reform congregation in our city for forty years.

Today this synagogue, "The Assembly of Israel" in English, is located just north of the city line, in Elkins Park, at 8339 Old York Road and Township Line Road. It is the largest of the six neighboring congregations on Old York Road and is larger than the six others found within a four-mile radius. As such, KI hosts many shared events.

Within it is the Meyers Library, containing over ten thousand books. It has several versions of the Talmud, reference books and children's books. It is primarily a Jewish library but does have a privately sponsored contemporary fiction collection. This section can be found for the most part on portable book racks that travel from the library to a room next to the sanctuary for borrowing and discussing during the Oneg Shabbat coffee and desserts after the Friday evening service.

The archive is another source of the congregation's pride, collecting and preserving records, photographs and documents of the congregation from the founding to the present. The archive begins with the minutes of the congregation's founding meeting. The collection contains over one million documents. The archive room, located off the library, draws numerous researchers and genealogists. It is open to the public once a week or by appointment.

Another KI institution is the Temple Judea Museum of religious objects and Jewish artwork, a separate area within the building located immediately inside the entrance of Keneseth Israel. It is self-supporting and independent of the synagogue. The museum was acquired by KI in 1982 when the venerable Temple Judea congregation was in decline and moved to a smaller home. Rita Poley, who has been the museum curator since 1999, suggests KI was chosen to house the collection because of its good exhibition

A modern Elijah Chair commissioned by Temple Judea Museum, Elkins Park. *Temple Judea Museum.*

space and because KI's rabbi at the time both appreciated and collected Jewish objects himself. The museum today hosts three changing exhibitions each year, including one dedicated to an Israeli topic. A second exhibition features items from the museum's collection of ritual objects, commissioned objects (see the Elijah Chair), fabric and ephemera. The third annual exhibition features works by the KI Artists Collaborative, formed in 2006 to promote the artistic presence of its talented member artists.

Indeed, KI is dedicated to promoting art and culture, serving the entire community with its arts, music and theatre series and adult education program. KI rabbi Lance Sussman, who teaches history at various universities, is one of Philadelphia's most popular and respected lecturers.

Another outstanding component of KI are the stained-glass windows created by noted artist Jacob Landau on the theme of the Prophetic Quest. When a KI committee was considering the commission for Landau in 1972, he was already an established artist, with work in New York's Museum of Modern Art, the Metropolitan Museum and the Philadelphia Museum of Art. He was also known for his portrayals of noted tragedies of the twentieth century, such as the Great Depression, the bombing of Hiroshima and the Holocaust. But the KI committee had to overcome concerns that the artist had never worked with glass nor had ever undertaken synagogue installations. Committee members apparently were also taken aback by the designs he submitted. In a letter to KI, Landau was forced to defend the unsmiling faces he portrays, stating, "The Prophets were not happy people."

In the end, Landau got the job, and it is wonderful that he did. Landau painted his images with subtle transparent watercolors. These sinuous washes were then translated into glass by stained-glass artist Benoit Gilsoul and then crafted and installed by the local Willet Hauser Studio. The remarkable collaboration took only two and a half years, a remarkably short time for such a task.

The windows are at their most glorious during the High Holidays, when the autumn light sets them aglow. They certainly contribute to the introspective mood of the service. The words of the Bible, both in Hebrew and in English, create forms dancing around the somber prophets, sometimes violent, sometimes tender and always intense.

In addition to its outstanding archives and artwork, KI has a history of outstanding rabbis. Indeed, KI has had only nine senior rabbis since its founding.

David Einhorn (1809–1879) is called the intellectual leader of American Reform Judaism. He had been the chief rabbi of Germany but was eventually barred from his pulpit for conducting services in the vernacular rather than in Hebrew. In addition, he had rejected prayers for the restoration of the Temple in Jerusalem, as well as for the restoration of Zion. It was not his intention, but he had completely alienated himself from his coreligionists. So, in 1855, off he went with his wife and nine children to Baltimore, filled with hope and promise and strong beliefs.

Baltimore, however, was very proslavery. Einhorn held that Jews, having been slaves in Egypt, should abhor slavery and added that owning slaves was a disgrace. He said that those who supported slavery put money before their values. Einhorn soon crossed the Mason-Dixon line and became rabbi of Keneseth Israel. That was the perfect choice. Though the congregation supported both political parties, it was unified in its opposition to slavery. Philadelphia welcomed Einhorn. He was quickly made an honorary member of the Union League, the patriotic society formed to promote the policies of Abraham Lincoln. Einhorn served as KI's rabbi from 1861 to 1866.

In the spirit of Reform, Einhorn rejected the divine authority of the Talmud. He published his own prayer book, *Olat Tamid* (Eternal Sacrifice), which deemphasized Israel and nationhood, removed

The Prophet Amos by Jacob Landau, Congregation Keneseth Israel Synagogue.
Willet Hauser Architectural Glass Studio, Inc.

the mention of the Messiah and eliminated references to sacrificial practices. His book would become the model for the Reform Movement's Union Prayer Book. Liberal as he was, however, Einhorn would not sanction intermarriage. Marrying outside the faith, he felt, was a nail in the coffin of the Jewish people. Einhorn maintained that as the Chosen People Jews had a special relationship with God.

Einhorn was succeeded by Dr. Samuel Hirsh, the former chief rabbi of Luxembourg and author of many books about Hegel. When Hirsh retired in 1886, Prussian-born Joseph Krauskopf (1858–1923) was invited to replace him. Krauskopf deliberated for quite a while. He feared following such notable predecessors. But that proved to be an unfounded fear. He served the congregation from 1887 to shortly before his death in 1923.

When Krauskopf arrived at KI, the congregation had 298 members. By 1890, the congregation numbered 2,500, an indication that Krauskopf was much loved and respected. But like Einhorn, he likewise introduced some radical ideas. We will soon learn how the historic Orthodox Mikveh Israel Synagogue fined members who worked on Shabbat. To circumvent this problem, Krauskopf moved the Sabbath service to Sunday. He said one can respect the spirit of the Bible but did not feel that one had to take it literally. Community relations, he opined, superseded the clock. This idea rattled many traditional congregants, but they stood by him.

Another notion would alienate members more—the removal of all signs of Jewish ethnicity. For Krauskopf, the Jews had evolved and should no longer be regarded as a nation but solely as a religious community. In line with Einhorn's thinking, references to Israel and the people of Israel were removed from the prayer book. (I wonder how both rabbis lived with the name "Keneseth Israel"?) It was his belief that the Jews were a people before receiving the land of Israel. He therefore opposed *political* Zionism but endorsed *spiritual* Zionism. Zionist flags were found in other synagogues, but at KI they were replaced by the American flag. This practice was extended to other Reform congregations when it was adopted at the Pittsburgh Central Conference of American Rabbis in July 1895, where Krauskopf was the platform chairman. This idea was expanded in Montreal in 1897. The Reform stance stated, "Here is the home of religious liberty, and we have aided in the founding of this new Zion... America is our Zion."

Krauskopf also founded the Patriotic Society of Philadelphia in 1910, the first of many chapters that aimed to instill a bond among citizens of Philadelphia and to work toward the city's betterment. He noted, "It was high time to put an end to the habit of seeing only that which is evil in Philadelphia and ignoring the far larger amounts of good...It is time that we crowd out the evil by developing more and more of that which is good."

Einhorn came from a family of rabbis, but Krauskopf's father had a lumber business in Prussia. Young Joseph had spent many days with his father in the forests. There he developed a love of nature and a strong interest in agriculture. This led him to found the Delaware Valley Farm School in Doylestown, Pennsylvania, in 1896. This college still thrives today. The decision to found this college was brought about during Krauskopf's visit to Russia in 1894, which included an extended visit with the novelist and social visionary Leo Tolstoy.

Krauskopf originally traveled to Russia to promote the establishment of a large farm cooperative community for survivors of pogroms. Krauskopf met for eight days at Tolstoy's ancestral farm estate to advance the idea of Russian Jews becoming farmers. The two took long walks, during which Tolstoy asked the rabbi many questions concerning the Jewish religion and the Jewish view of Christianity. Apparently, there was a genuine meeting of the minds. But when Krauskopf broached the idea of a Jewish farming community near Odessa, Tolstoy said that it would make more sense to found a Jewish farming community in America, where both the fertile soil and religious freedom would help Jews flourish. He added that the Russian Church and the tsars would never support Jewish agricultural settlements. Leave the ghettos of Europe, Tolstoy advised, and form a farm school in America.

The Delaware Valley Farm School was duly founded by Krauskopf and his friends as a nonsectarian institution but with a goal of encouraging Jewish lads to follow the honorable, useful and

Tolstoy meets Krauskopf. *Delaware Valley College.*

independent calling of agriculture. The original board members came mainly from the KI community, and so it is today. The charter reads that the purpose of the school is to train youth to become scientific and practical agriculturists. Krauskopf at first had difficulty raising funds for the school. He wryly noted, "I learned then what I have learned many times since, that when money is needed for a good cause, nothing is given as liberally as advice."

Part II

THE WALKING TOUR

Ben and Linda conferring at the University of Pennsylvania. *Photograph by Matt Nesvisky.*

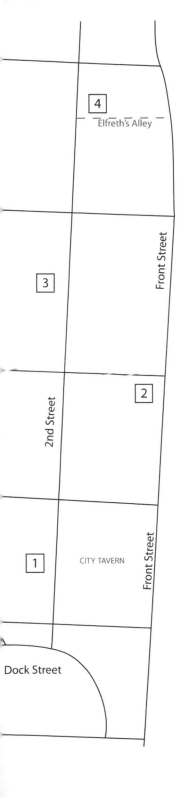

1. Welcome Park

2. London Coffee House

3. Christ Church

4. Elfreth's Alley

5. Christ Church Cemetery

6. Mikveh Israel

7. NMAJH

8. Liberty Bell

9. Mikveh Israel Cemetery

1. WELCOME PARK

The small and little-visited Welcome Park is a logical place to begin our tour. Located on Second Street, between Chestnut and Walnut Streets and opposite the historic City Tavern, this space is dedicated to William Penn, the founder of our city and state. The park was created by local architect Robert Venturi, who favors incorporating words and slogans on exterior building spaces. He does so here with the illustrated biography of William Penn on the park's southern enclosure wall.

Welcome was the name of Penn's ship, which transported him here from England in 1682. On this very plot of ground Penn rented a home from a fellow Quaker, Samuel Carpenter. Because of its roof, the house was called "the Slate House," a model of which is shown on a pedestal in the rear or eastern side of the park. In the Slate House, Penn mapped the grid plan of our city, two square miles "river to river."

Look down where you're standing. A sixty-foot map, based on Penn's original sketch of 1682 and complete with street names still used today, is engraved on the pavement and set between the bas-reliefs of our Schuylkill River to the west and Delaware River to the east. The four decorative pear tree planters represent Penn's original four city parks, which eventually became known as Washington Square, Rittenhouse Square, Franklin Square and Logan Square. The statue of Penn, a scale model of the thirty-seven-foot sculpture atop City Hall tower, indicates Center Square. Penn is holding "The Charter of Privileges," which he drafted in 1701 granting freedom of religion to all. That charter, which remained the constitutional framework of colonial Pennsylvania until 1776, would prove to be a document of great importance to Jews, dissident Christian sects and others who could not practice their religion freely in the Old World.

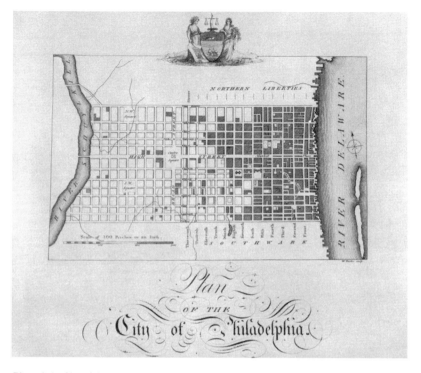

Plan of the City of Philadelphia, by Thomas Holme, 1682. *Library of Congress.*

To commemorate the charter's fiftieth anniversary, the nearby Liberty Bell was commissioned in 1751 from the Whitechapel Foundry in London.

Penn chose the name "Philadelphia" after an ancient Greek colony (where today stands Amman, the capital of the Hashemite Kingdom of Jordan). Philadelphia in Greek means "one who loves his brother"—hence the City of Brotherly Love, as residents refer to it today. For Penn, a deeply religious man, the designation of Philadelphia was not chosen lightly. He hoped to establish what would be a utopia of its time, a place where people of all faiths could mingle freely and thrive together in harmony. No place in Europe came close to such an ideal. Penn had even communicated his idea to the local Delaware Leni-Lenape nation before he ever set foot in the New World and was able to create a lasting bond with the

Delaware River front, engraving. *Library of Congress.*

Native Americans from the start, signing a pact with the trustworthy Chief Tamanend.

Penn came to the New World seeking religious expression without fear of incarceration. He had in fact been imprisoned in England for being a Quaker, or more properly, a member of the Society of Friends; at that time England's only recognized faith was Anglicanism. The great tract of New World acreage had originally been given to his father, Admiral William Penn (who was an Anglican, not a Quaker), in payment for services to King Charles II. The son named the territory Pennsylvania—Penn's Woods—after his recently deceased father, and Philadelphia was to be a "Holy Experiment" in religious tolerance. The era between 1682 and 1726 was to be known as the Quaker Golden Age in Pennsylvania.

While Penn welcomed all religions, he held the Jews in special regard; he also hoped to proselytize them because they did not accept Jesus. Until they did so, he believed that the messianic age could not come about. Yet he did respect the Jews. Like himself, he recognized the Jews as victims of religious intolerance. He noted, too, that both Quakers and Jews were loath to take oaths. He also saw resemblances between Jews and the Indians he admired. He believed that the Indians were descendants of the Ten Lost Tribes. According to Penn, both had "ruddy" complexions and dark hair and eyes; their festivals were based on lunar calendars, and both celebrated first fruit festivals. Penn looked with favor on all of this. While the Puritans up in Boston viewed the Indians as cohorts of the devil, Penn regarded the Indians with high esteem.

Penn had been drawn to the Quaker religion at age twenty-two. He was attracted to the concept of silent meditation that, when successful, could lead to achieving an "inner light." This has parallels among kabbalists and other mystics. George Fox, the founder of the Society of Friends, shared with Penn the messianic fervor to create a utopian society in which all could practice their religion freely. You might say that this goal was realized. Unlike a city such as colonial Boston, which was almost exclusively Puritan, Penn's Philadelphia was a religious and ethnic melting pot, and it remains so today. In the

Welcome Park, with the William Penn statue in the center. *Photograph by author.*

colonial period, Penn's "Holy Experiment" was a tapestry of English Protestants, Dutch Calvinists, Irish Catholics, German Lutherans, Scandinavian Swedenborgians and Portuguese Jews; today you can add everything from Vietnamese Buddhists to Senegalese Muslims to the mix.

Penn's desire to create a harmonious and orderly city extended to his physical plan for Philadelphia—a grid concept developed by the Romans. The grid he mapped with surveyor Thomas Holmes was 12.5 miles wide, extending from the bank of the Delaware (which is just a few blocks behind Welcome Park) to the Schuylkill. This grid was also practical. Penn was cognizant of the Great Fire of London of 1666, fifteen years before Penn's first trip to America in 1682. Although Penn and his family were living in Ireland at the time of the great conflagration (fortunately, for Pennsylvanians!), Penn would have known that London had been reduced to ashes largely due to the difficulty of firefighters struggling to get through the city's labyrinth of congested streets.

Hence the neat, geometric grid of the Welcome Park map. While you study the Penn biography on the southern edge of the map, think of how word of William Penn's promised land of religious freedom eventually spread throughout the Jewish world. By the 1800s, the southern sector of Philadelphia had become home to an ever-growing Jewish community—a little Lower East Side. Here Yiddish was spoken, and a Yiddish press served the influx of Eastern and Central European Jewish immigrants. The neighborhood even included a number of bohemian poets and writers. Henrietta Szold, who established Hadassah, the women's Zionist organization, resided here. She was also a young editor of the Jewish Publication Society, which was founded in Philadelphia in 1888. Today, JPS is the oldest Jewish publishing house in America. Another notable resident of South Philly, at least temporarily, was the peripatetic poet Naphtali Hertz Imbar, who in 1877 composed the Hebrew lyrics of "Hatikvah," the Zionist national anthem.

Now pace along the map until your feet find Spruce Street. There, near Fifth Street, the renowned Rebecca Gratz directed an orphanage. The Mikveh Israel Cemetery—established in 1740 before the synagogue of the same name itself was erected—is located at Spruce and Ninth Streets, opposite the Pennsylvania Hospital, the first hospital in the colonies.

The Center Square, where our impressive City Hall is positioned, straddles Center City's two widest avenues: Broad Street (Fourteenth Street), which runs north to south, and High Street, going west to east. The High Street of Penn's day, however, is today called Market Street. But it's still Philly's main commercial street.

Numbered streets extended north–south, with the odd numbers going north and even numbers, south. Streets bearing names extended east–west. But notice here that these streets are not named after people—the Quakers were too modest to name streets after themselves or their fellows. Instead, streets were assigned innocuous names, often after fruit trees, such as Walnut, Chestnut, Filbert, Cherry, Locust, Pine and so on. School House Lane and Meeting House Road, meanwhile, indicated institutions required in all Quaker communities. Regarding their school system, the Quakers established a high standard of education. To this very day, parents of numerous religious backgrounds, including Jewish parents, enroll their children in Philadelphia's elite and highly regarded Friends' school system.

Another example of Quaker modesty, by the way, is reflected in how they regarded entertainment. Philadelphia's venerable music hall, for example, was named the "Academy of Music," rather than the "Opera House." Such nomenclature, along with the street names, still reflects the Penn/Quaker imprint here.

The City of Brotherly Love was one of only two planned cities in the colonies—that is, drawn up before they were built. The other is Savannah, Georgia, planned in 1733 by James Oglethorpe. Philadelphia's street map was completed by William Penn in 1682. With only a few exceptions, such as expressway ramps and underground transportation, our colonial city plan remains largely unchanged, much to the frustration of tour bus operators trying to move their vehicles along what are often, at best, two-lane streets.

Penn desired to create not only a tolerant city but also one populated by well-read and educated residents. For this reason, Penn appointed James Logan as his city administrator during Penn's second and final stay here in 1701. (Penn never settled permanently in the New World, reportedly because his wife preferred England and because they believed their sickly child would get better treatment there.) Logan was a multilingual scholar who, among other things, possessed the largest Hebrew library in the colonies. Included in his nearly three-thousand-volume collection was an impressive Hebraic library. Logan owned the complete six volumes of the Mishneh Torah by Moses Maimonides, written in the twelfth century; many rare Hebrew Bibles; and the Shulchan Aruch, the code of Jewish law written by kabbalist Rabbi Joseph Karo in Safed during the sixteenth century.

Speaking of kabbalists, although countless books have been written about William Penn, none that I know of considers a provocative parallel to his mystical vision of a "Holy Experiment" that may well have come to his attention in his youth. Now as we stand below Penn's statue in Welcome Park, let's contemplate what may have been a strong Jewish component that contributed to his beliefs.

In 1655, the philosopher and kabbalist Rabbi Menasseh ben Israel left Holland for London on a mission: to persuade Oliver

Cromwell to allow Jews to settle in England for the first time since their expulsion from Britain in 1290 by King Edward I.

Menasseh ben Israel brought with him his book, *The Hope of Israel* (1650). This book was written in response to the Cossack pogroms in Poland of 1648. In the book, the rabbi expressed his fervent dream of a Jewish homeland, a safe place "somewhere, where the Jewish people could live in peace and practice their religion without secrecy." Menasseh ben Israel spent two years in London. Besides discussing his ideas with Oliver Cromwell, he addressed Parliament and circulated his ideas in numerous meetings among the aristocracy and others of the ruling class. The Penns, of course, were members of the upper class. The young William Penn, a student at the Chigwell School, was definitely in London the same time the mystical rabbi was making his rounds in the city. Penn could have heard Menasseh ben Israel speak in his family's home or may have heard the rabbi spoken about by his father, the admiral.

Menasseh ben Israel (his very name suggesting his proto-Zionism) was born in Lisbon in 1604, a descendant of Spanish Marranos. He eventually settled in Amsterdam, where he established a Hebrew printing house and became chief rabbi, greatly renowned for his oratory. He established a Talmud Torah school and taught, among others, Baruch Spinoza. Spinoza was known to have Quaker contacts. He lived in the same neighborhood as Rembrandt, and Menasseh ben Israel and the artist became friends. Rembrandt immortalized the rabbi in drawings, four etchings and a painting, all found in the British Museum.

In 1644, Menasseh ben Israel traveled to South America. While there, he met a Jewish immigrant named Antonio de Montezinos, who conveyed to the rabbi the belief that Andean natives were descendants of the Ten Lost Tribes of Israel. Did that idea, along with the rabbi's fervor (for religious tolerance, for a Promised Land, for silent meditation as a means to achieving an "inner light"), reach the ears of twelve-year-old William Penn during Menasseh ben Israel's visit to England? Might such notions have been the catalyst for the "Holy Experiment" Penn sought to create in Philadelphia twenty-eight years later?

We do know that William Penn wrote of having a mystical experience when he was thirteen, shortly after Menasseh ben Israel's visit to London. Elsewhere in his writings, he discusses his concept of ethical mysticism, advocating withdrawal from the world in order to commune with God and then a return to the world to do God's work, such as creating a city of perfect harmony (i.e., Philadelphia). Such a notion parallels Jewish kabbalists' concept of "Tikkun Olam"—repairing the world. Penn, incidentally, twice visited the Netherlands, where Menasseh ben Israel was chief rabbi. Admittedly, my Penn–ben Israel connection is speculative, but when I discussed it with Professor of Jewish Mysticism Joel Hecker, he said that the theory was well worth pursuing—and I hope some scholar will indeed pursue the matter. Who knows, but for a kabbalistic rabbi, might we not have this statue of William Penn before us today in Welcome Park?

Across the street from the park, by the way, we see the City Tavern. This was the "watering hole" used by our founding fathers as a place

City Tavern. *Library of Congress.*

Inside the City Tavern. *City Tavern.*

to meet and informally debate the details of the U.S. Constitution. Meticulously reconstructed after a fire some years back, the City Tavern is currently operated by the National Park Service. Here visitors can have a glimpse of life in the Revolutionary War period, with waitstaff dressed in colonial garb who serve authentic period dishes and brews and with pewter crockery, goblets and cutlery.

In the corner building to the left of the tavern once stood a market managed by the Gratz brothers, Barnard and Michael, who were among the most prominent and successful of Philadelphia's first Jews. They rented their shop from the Quaker Isaac Norris, the man who chose the passage from Deuteronomy that is inscribed on the Liberty Bell.

Leaving the Welcome Park and the City Tavern area, let's now walk north on Second Street for two blocks and then turn right on Market Street. Continue for one block. Here you'll come to Front Street, on the other side of which is the Delaware River, with Camden, New Jersey, on the opposite shore. The otherwise anonymous commercial building on the corner where you're standing occupies a site significant to our tour. Granted, the surrounding traffic is almost too noisy to let you think. Nonetheless, it's now time to consider a prominent Jew of the Revolutionary War period: Haym Salomon.

2. HAYM SALOMON

The trend these days is to underplay Haym Salomon's role in financing the American Revolution. My readings persuade me otherwise. He was indeed a most significant player. We will soon see that he was an honorable and skilled commodities broker, a dedicated Patriot and a generous benefactor. Under extreme pressure, coupled within extreme time constraints, he took great personal risks for the newly emerging nation when others much wealthier than he would not. He simply could not say "no." George Washington and Robert Morris depended on him, and he always managed to meet their endless demands to raise more and more money. He worked against the clock. He drove himself and ignored his poor health, suffering coughing bouts, hemorrhages and great pain. His patriotic zeal, in fact, would lead him to an early grave.

Salomon was born in Leszno (Lissa), Poland, in 1740 to Sephardic parents ("Sepharad" is the Hebrew name for Spain). He was the son of a rabbi. Salomon witnessed considerable persecution of Jews, including an act of arson that destroyed the Jewish quarter of his town. He left Leszno shortly before the partition of Poland, when King Stanislaw II instituted heavy taxes and even heavier levies on Jews. Not wishing to be a burden on his family, he left them in 1764. He traveled throughout Europe, studying, working, mastering seven languages and honing his business skills, particularly regarding exchange in currencies. It is also assumed that during this period he became totally disenchanted with rule by the old monarchies of Europe—and subsequently enamored of the idea of a democratic republic in the New World.

After nearly six years of wandering, Salomon arrived in New York in 1772, shortly after the Battles of Lexington and Concord. He was thirty-two and eager for life in the New World. Salomon soon became a supporter of American independence. He joined the Sons of Liberty—an organization that, among other things, raised money for the formation and provisioning of the Continental army. The organization also proposed boycotting English goods and was responsible for the Boston Tea Party in December 1773.

That act of rebellion, as well as his business dealings with the colonists' French allies, led the British to suspect that Salomon was a spy. They twice imprisoned him and once even sentenced him to be hanged. But it was Salomon's knowledge of German that saved him from execution; the British found him invaluable as an interpreter for their Hessian mercenaries, and his hanging was deferred indefinitely. During his incarceration in damp and miserable cells, it is believed that Salomon contracted tuberculosis. While he survived, many did not.

His first jail, known as the Old Sugar House in lower Manhattan, had a collapsed roof. Rain would enter, and dysentery, typhus, tuberculosis and cholera claimed countless lives. Later he was sent to Bridewell Prison, also located in lower Manhattan, which was even worse than the Sugar House. Bridewell Prison became known as Provost Prison, because the provost, or prison commandant, would reserve all the fresh food for himself, leaving only moldy bread and other spoiled food for the prisoners. The poor conditions of each prison, coupled with his obsessive drive for work, were responsible for Salomon's death at age forty-five.

While in jail, Salomon ironically did become something of a spy. As the British were exploiting their prisoner for his language skills, Salomon was for many months acquiring intelligence on British military plans. He was also instrumental in helping American and French prisoners escape jail, even providing them with money and food. Via these escaped prisoners Salomon was able to pass on British plans to the Continental army.

His own escape was quite daring. He persuaded his jailer, a Hessian mercenary, that his life would be better if he threw in his lot with the Americans, adding that General George Washington himself was seeking Hessian deserters. Salomon sweetened the deal by bribing the guard with his gold watch and orchestrated their separate escapes. Salomon persuaded his jailer to leave his cell unlocked. Then, an hour after the Hessian had deserted his post, Salomon made his own run for it. Weakened by consumption and malnourishment, he nevertheless managed to elude the pursuing dogs by wading through streams. It was a harrowing experience.

When Salomon made it to the American lines, he was shocked by the conditions of the ragtag soldiers. This sight inspired his mission in life: to help the troops so that they would be victorious and make the United States an independent nation. He knew he had to leave New York immediately; the British were close behind him. He couldn't even risk saying goodbye to his wife and child. He fled to Philadelphia.

When he arrived in Philadelphia, he found himself among friends at the Mikveh Israel Synagogue. They were in awe of his escape. They fed and clothed him and planned his reunion with his wife and child in Philadelphia. His fellow Jews eventually provided Salomon funds to begin a small business and suggested that he petition the Continental Congress for a position in recompense for the service he had rendered to the American cause. Congress turned down

Wharf at Penn's Landing, engraving. *Library of Congress.*

his request. Undaunted, Salomon set to work, initially as a distiller. Soon his language skills and knowledge of European commodities were bringing him success in the import-export business.

Salomon kept one brokerage office in his home and another in an early stock exchange called the London Coffee House, which was located right where we're standing now, by the Delaware Riverfront at Penn's Landing, on the corner of Front and Market Streets. Business hours were from 12:00 p.m. to 2:00 p.m. The handsome London Coffee House stood until 1854 and no longer exists, but the drawing from the Library Company of Philadelphia shows how it looked.

An advertisement of Salomon's that appeared in a local paper on February 28, 1781, mentions "a few bills to exchange from France, St. Eustacea, and Amsterdam." Salomon traded in numerous commodities but on principle did not deal in the slave trade, as many brokers did.

In 1781, Robert Morris was appointed superintendent of the Office of Finance, the pre-Constitution equivalent of U.S. Treasury secretary. Morris was soon calling on Salomon for help in straightening out the colonies' muddled financial affairs and low credit rating. He even turned to Salomon to contribute funds to establish his bank, the Bank of North America. This institution was established toward the end of the war to control the rapidly devaluing American currency. It would be some time before Americans would have a credible national currency. At Morris's request, Salomon donated $900 to get the bank going. Morris was keen to involve Salomon in the bank because nations such as France and Germany held him in high esteem. Soon enough, those nations began investing in the bank. France, for example, loaned it $2 million. Slowly the currency began to rise in value, and the country could cover its bills. Stores once more accepted paper money.

Salomon, meanwhile, had reinforced his standing as a backer of the Patriot cause when he extended interest-free loans and subsidies to members of the Continental Congress, including Thomas Jefferson and James Madison. Madison's diary in the National Archives contains over seventy references to Salomon, crediting him with supplying badly needed blankets, guns, bullets, food and uniforms for the underfinanced troops. Madison also

London Coffee House. *Library Company of Philadelphia.*

refers to his "quiet benefactor," Haym Salomon, and to Madison's "mortification" at having to request such personal financial assistance. But he also notes that Salomon rejected recompense in any form. Salomon aided those founding fathers because he knew that in serving the budding republic, such men were neglecting their domestic affairs and were often short of money—money that the Continental Congress could not provide. Salomon also provided financial support to Europeans who had aided the Revolution, such as Baron Friedrich von Steuben and Colonel Andrzej Kościuszko.

Robert Morris had been reluctant at first to ask a Jewish broker for money, but General Washington, desperate and disappointed by the failure of states to fulfill their financial commitments for the cause, personally urged Morris to turn to Salomon, whom he admired and trusted. Morris actually knocked on the door of Mikveh Israel Synagogue on Yom Kippur, not realizing the solemnity of the day, to ask Haym Salomon to raise funds for the cause. To the amazement of the congregation, Salomon stood up and stressed the importance of contributing to the emerging nation. His dramatic appeal yielded $20,000 in less than a quarter of an hour, a business kept brisk so the congregation could return to prayer. (Such fundraising was customary for Salomon, who was so persistent in seeking donations "for the good of the nation" that his friends began to avoid him, even crossing the street rather than cross paths.)

Robert Morris valued Salomon for his financial acumen, for his contacts in France (then the Americans' chief European ally) and for his spotless reputation. There were some twenty-five commodity brokers at the time, of whom two (Salomon and Moses Cohen) were Jewish. But unlike the other brokers, Salomon had never defaulted on a loan or broken an agreement. He was known to take risks when others would not but made good even when some notes proved worthless. He also charged the lowest interest rate—0.5 percent—when it was common to charge 2 to 5 percent. Salomon believed—correctly, as it turned out—that he would make up his earnings in volume of trade.

Morris began to rely on Salomon so much that he created a position for him as "broker to the house of finance," something like an assistant to the secretary of treasury. Salomon took the job but continued his private enterprises as well. Today this would likely inspire cries of conflict of interest and might well be illegal. Nevertheless, Morris and others in the government considered Salomon's services invaluable. Defying his doctor's orders to rest, he worked day and night to accumulate money for the war effort. In *Early American Jewry*, Jacob Rader Marcus estimated that Salomon raised over $800,000 for the newly emerging nation. The sum, calculated as of 2005 using relative share of GDP, which indicates purchasing power, equaled $40 billion, or about $49 billion in

Heald Square Monument of President Washington holding the hands of Robert Morris and Haym Salomon, sculpture by Lorado Taft. *City of Chicago Public Collections.*

2010. He performed this feat in less than ten years. The man was a financial genius.

Even as other brokers moved up the ladder and to grander quarters outside the port area, Salomon continued to live modestly. Yet he always gave to causes that he held dear, like the Mikveh Israel

Synagogue, providing 25 percent of the building budget in 1782 for the synagogue's Cherry Street location.

In addition, Salomon sent money to his family back in Poland. His downfall began when a plan emerged for a major private bank that would compete with the Bank of North America, which had been chartered by an act of Congress. This bank was located on Chestnut Street, west of Third Street. Here Morris and Salomon conducted the government's business. Miers Fisher, a Quaker lawyer with Tory sympathies, supported the new Bank of Pennsylvania in 1783. In a newspaper attack, Fisher libeled the "Jew broker" Salomon. Clearly, Fisher's classic anti-Semitic tactic was meant to divert attention from himself, as Fisher's interest charges were four and a half times greater than Salomon's.

Fisher had made his fortune selling goods to the British and had even spied for the Crown in order to receive its business. Salomon answered Fisher's libels with the help of Editor Eleazer Oswald of the *Independent Gazetteer* vigorously defending the Jews' patriotism and furiously attacking the Quakers for not supporting the Patriots in their time of need. To Fisher's accusation of Jewish usury, Salomon riposted, "Thou art the man."

Sadly, both Salomon and Morris died deeply in debt. Indeed, when Salomon died in 1785, his assets barely covered his liabilities. Haym Salomon had also been a victim of his generosity. Many times he gave people outright grants. At other times he extended loans, such as to the Continental Congress and army, at little or no interest, and usually not even the principal was repaid to Salomon. His longtime assistant, a Scot named McCrae, had repeatedly warned his employer that with all his grants and loans he was writing his financial death sentence, and he further cautioned that the man was working himself to death. McCrae also complained to Rachel Salomon of her husband's lavish generosity.

When Salomon died, an obituary notice in the *Independent Gazetteer* read, "Thursday last, expired, after a lingering illness, Mr. Haym Salomon, an eminent Broker of this city. He was a native of Poland, and of the Hebrew nation. He was remarkable for his skill, and integrity in his profession, and for his generous and humane deportment. His remains were yesterday deposited in the burial

Tamanend at Penn's Landing, by sculptor Raymond Sandoval. *Photograph by Joey Blue.*

ground of the synagogue, in this city." In the Mikveh Israel Cemetery, which we visit later, a plaque notes that Salomon's "wizardry with money is reputed to have rescued the US from defeat during the war."

Salomon died believing some $350,000 was owed by the government to his wife and young children. Despite Rachel Salomon's efforts, no money was ever paid to her or to her descendants. Two years after Haym's death, Rachel married David Heilbrum, apparently a Scottish Jew, perhaps as much out of need as by choice.

Now back to our noisy twenty-first-century street corner. Across the street from the site of the London Coffee House and next to the bridge, you'll note a large and somewhat mysterious sculpture. Erected in 1995, the sculpture is of Tamanend, the Leni-Lenape Indian chieftain who signed the peace treaty with William Penn. The signing ceremony took place nearby at what is now called Penn's Landing, the spot on the Delaware River at which Penn disembarked in 1682.

Tamanend stands on a turtle, representing Mother Earth. On his shoulder perches an eagle, the messenger of the Great Spirit. Because his name was synonymous throughout the colonies with trust and probity, New York Democrats named their headquarters Tammany Hall after him in 1789. A few feet away from the site of the Coffee House, by the Chestnut Street corner, was Pemberton Wharf. This wharf was used by the merchant Nathan Levy, who among other things received delivery of the Liberty Bell here. The

Gratz family merchants also used this wharf. To see an expanse of the Delaware River and to visualize colonial America's number-one port, turn right on Front Street (note the blue and gold London Coffee House historical marker) and walk one short block to Chestnut. Cross the street and continue along the pedestrian bridge for a great view of the Delaware River.

The dreaded yellow fever epidemic began in this region in 1793, imported here by mosquitoes and/or slaves brought from the Caribbean. Nearly four thousand Philadelphians died of the disease, an average of seventy per day. Considering that the population of the city was fifty-five thousand, this epidemic was one of the most devastating in American history. During the winter, however, the mosquitoes died off and the epidemic was over.

The eminent colonial physician Benjamin Rush believed that bleeding was a cure, but of course this only achieved the opposite effect. While vast numbers of Rush's patients died, Jewish physician David de Isaac Nassy managed to save most of those under his care. Of his more than 160 patients, only 19 died. His prescription for recovery was threefold: avoid crowds, take frequent vinegar baths and wear a camphor bag around the neck. This was a sophisticated idea for the time for the treatment of contagious diseases, which no one understood. But Nassy had read his Hebrew Bible, in which this regimen was set forth in the Book of Leviticus.

Nassy had arrived in Philadelphia in 1792. He was a noted pharmacist and physician from Surinam. Within a short time of his arrival, he was elected a member of the esteemed American Philosophical Society. He was the first Jewish physician in Philadelphia. He joined Congregation Mikveh Israel, which had hardly any deaths from yellow fever, largely thanks to Nassy.

3. The Way to Elfreth's Alley

Leaving the riverfront, we head back westward along Market Street to Second Street. Cross Second and then turn right to cross Marke

Palladian window inside Christ Church. *Photograph by author.*

Just past the intersection you'll see an imposing church. You might not think that a church has a place on a Jewish tour, but think again. This is Christ Church, the graceful colonial-era edifice in which many of America's founding fathers worshipped.

On the Second Street side of this historic Anglican church is a lovely Palladian window. If it looks at all familiar, that's because there is an identical window at Independence Hall. The church proudly delights in its clear windows, which are unusual, since churches usually have stained glass. The idea was to allow a view of nature, and this particular window is framed by a flowering pear tree each spring.

So is there a Jewish connection? You bet. This restored window was a gift from a member of the Gimbel department store family, whose flagship store operated in Philadelphia from 1887 to 1986. To the right of this window inside the church, a brass plaque reads:

And God said, "Let there be light: and there was light."
The restoration of this window has been done in honor of the lasting
friendship between Congregation Mikveh Israel and Christ Church in
Philadelphia and made possible by a gift from Fridolyn Gimbel
Graham 5721 1960

And that's hardly the only reason we're stopping by a church.

Christ Church and the nearby Mikveh Israel Synagogue (which we'll visit soon) have a remarkable, shared history. During the early colonial days, money was scarce, yet each institution could count on the other in times of need. Indeed, having to relocate itself four times, Mikveh Israel received financial support from church congregants for each move. A further sign of friendship occurred with the ratification of the U.S. Constitution, when the church's Bishop William White and the synagogue's Hazan (Cantor) Jacob Raphael Cohen walked arm in arm in a jubilant parade down Market Street. Refreshment tables were laid with delicacies, and there was even a kosher food table.

Throughout the ensuing years, the two congregations would frequently share meals, often in connection with their mutual aid in periodic building or renovation projects. Sometime after World War II, according to synagogue archivist Dan Cohen, the two congregations instituted annual joint banquets for their congregants, held in early May. The congregations took turns playing host, and the church even had a complete kosher table setting. This tradition continues, although these days the kosher meals are supplied by a caterer and arrive with disposable dishes and cutlery.

In addition to finding Jewish history in a church, we can also find a source of Jewish pride just across the street...in a parking lot.

Opposite the church's Palladian window, in the parking lot, you can see one of the more than three thousand murals that brighten Philadelphia. The idea for such murals began as an attempt to displace and discourage graffiti scrawled on empty surfaces around town. The project was proposed by Jewish artist Jane Golden, who with much effort persuaded a doubtful city government to give her the green light in the early 1980s. She and a small group of artists (armed with a correspondingly small budget) began to work with the

Parks and Recreation Department to convince street gangs to put down their aerosol cans and to take up paint brushes. The idea was to celebrate neighborhoods rather than to deface them. The program quickly became successful. It was featured in *National Geographic*, and through the years sponsorship and funding have continued to grow. Golden now heads a staff of very skilled artists, including thirty-six of the original street gang members involved. Despite the initial skepticism, the war against graffiti art has been largely won. As Golden states, "People in neighborhoods see graffiti as hopelessness. When they see a mural, they have community pride."

The mural we see here on Second Street is less than one story high. Others tower five stories and more. Some even employ mirrored glass, mosaics and found materials. This one, named *Fringe Festival Mural*, was painted by muralist Tom Judd in 1999. It captures the spirit of the city's fringe arts festival, held annually in this area, with random images—"chance associations juxtaposing unrelated images," according to the artist.

Now continuing north on Second Street for about two blocks, we turn right shortly before the Ben Franklin Bridge to visit unique little Elfreth's Alley, nestled on the very edge of our city—and of our state.

4. ELFRETH'S ALLEY

Elfreth's Alley has the distinction of being the oldest continuously inhabited residential street in America, and as such the entire street is a National Historic Landmark site. In an exception to the Quaker custom of not naming streets after individuals, the little lane acquired its designation because of an eighteenth-century blacksmith named Jeremiah Elfreth, the original owner of the property. Since that time, over three thousand residents have lived here. The alley is located in the Old City section of Philadelphia, a short block from the Delaware River. The earliest home dates from 1702. Thirty-two homes exist here today. The entrance is on Second Street, between Arch and Race Streets.

Elfreth's Alley, the oldest continuously inhabited street in America. *Photograph by author.*

Although well marked, this charming street is still easy to overlook, tiny and tucked away and overshadowed as it is. As the city grew throughout the centuries, the historical areas became totally intertwined with modern Philadelphia. This is not, after all, a showpiece community like Williamsburg, Virginia.

Here are some tips for identifying an early colonial period structure. The brick pattern, known as a Flemish bond, consists of headers (bricks set lengthwise into the wall) and spacers (bricks laid horizontally), usually in a red and black pattern, although sometimes all red. The color is less important, because the walls were not built to be decorative but functional. The colonists were arriving from England during the beginning of the eighteenth century, and many had witnessed the devastation of the Great Fire of London of 1666. Arriving in a settlement without a municipal police force or fire department, the colonists used this type of brickwork for thicker, more insulated walls. This, however required more materials and more expense. As the city develope the homeowners began to economize by using only spacers. This is the most noticeable clue to look for as one searches for other historical structures around town. Meanwhile, the shared exterior wall design of the homes on Elfreth's Alley set a pattern for the working-class row house neighborhoods that would eventually become a feature of many American cities.

Related to the brick are the fire plaques on the second- or third-story walls. These were essentially fire insurance policies. They identified which of the three private fire companies that patrolled town with horse-drawn water wagons and leather buckets was obligated to service a particular home should the home catch fire. You will not see these plaques on homes built after this early period, when the municipality finally assumed the task of firefighting. Today such plaques are collector's items sold in antique stores.

Another distinction of Elfreth's Alley is the cobblestone paving designed for horse and carriage, with the smooth bordering stones for the wheels and the cobblestone part for the horse. Think practical. A horse would have a call of nature from time to time,

Fire plaques at Carpenter's Hall. *Photograph by author.*

and the rough stones would be a lot less slippery for pedestrians to cross than smooth slabs of stone.

Now note the small, intimate streetlights, four-sided and designed to be easily opened and filled with oil. Contrast them with the taller streetlights of today. Theses oil lamps can be found throughout the older sections of town. And lastly, notice the curious, mirrored viewing devices posted outside second-floor windows. They are called busy bodies. With these lamps, colonial residents could easily (and discreetly) keep tabs on all the comings and goings on the street. It was also a security device employed in the days without police protection.

You can do a little snooping yourself by peeping at the beautiful little rear gardens many of these homes have. But just peep from the street and don't go beyond the gates, as these homes are, after all, private residences.

A visit to Elfreth's Alley provides an appreciation of the lifestyle of the day; thanks to its National Historic Landmark status, the integrity of the street is preserved. Current Elfreth's homeowners may paint their houses only with the colors used in colonial times and cannot adorn their exteriors with bay windows, stoops or decks. Inside the walls is another matter, and residents may have a Jacuzzi or a dishwasher or whatever else. With one or two exceptions, which occurred before its Historic Landmark status was established, this alleyway remains a perfect period piece. In fact, Elfreth's Alley has served as an outdoor set for numerous period films. Google lists over one thousand films produced in our city. Elfreth's Alley served as a location for many of them, with the 1997 movie version of Toni Morrison's *Beloved* perhaps the most notable.

The people who first occupied the lane's two-story homes were either tradesmen or tradeswomen (women did indeed own property then) or were craftspeople. Their shops were located on the ground floor, and they lived over the shops. The shops were owned by tailors, seamstresses, upholsterers, shoemakers, blacksmiths and so on. Prosperous residents added a third floor to their buildings. Today's units are sometimes expanded by breaking through interior walls. At present there are twenty-nine residential units and three more on the Bladden Court passageway off the alley.

But my Jewish readers may be impatiently demanding: where's the Israelite connection? Indeed, some Jewish families were among the very first to dwell in Elfreth's Alley. Jacob Cohen, for example, settled in the city in 1781, fleeing from Charleston after being released from a British prison there. He was a successful fur trader working the length of the "South" River (the Delaware), having received a license to do so from Britain's West India Company. Cohen purchased pelts from the Indians. He was known as a rather charismatic fellow, a rough-and-tumble frontiersman type. He was known to have corresponded with Daniel Boone concerning Kentucky's hunting and trading prospects. Legendary in his day, it is believed that Cohen was the inspiration for *Jacob and the Indians*, a 1939 novel by Pulitzer Prize–winning novelist Stephen Vincent Benét. Jacob Cohen's home, number 124, is currently the museum of the street.

Only a few homes away, at number 118, lived Moses Mordecai. While most properties on this street were owned by craftsmen, Mordecai was a merchant. He was born in Bonn, Germany, in 1707, later moving to England. There he was unsuccessful in business, could not pay his debts and was imprisoned. The British shipped him to America at age fifty-one as an indentured servant. When his servitude ended, he moved to Philadelphia shortly before 1762, where his son Jacob was born. Jacob would later become Haym Salomon's business partner. Mordecai had married Elizabeth (Esther) Whitlock, who converted to Judaism prior to their marriage. Mordecai was one of the founders of the Mikveh Israel Synagogue. He was a signer of the nonimportation resolutions of 1765 that challenged British authority in the colonies. By signing on to these resolutions, colonial merchants, and several Jews among them, went on record as refusing to accept any goods shipped from Great Britain until the Stamp Act and its hated tax were repealed. As a product of the Enlightenment, Mordecai supported the independence movement and later heartily endorsed the U.S. Constitution.

The neighboring Cohens and Mordecais became intertwined following the death of Moses Mordecai in 1781. His widow was destitute, could not pay her rent and appealed to the Mikveh

Israel congregants for help in 1782. Cohen was still a bachelor at age thirty-six and wanted to settle down. He thereupon courted Mordecai's widow. Hazan Gershom Mendes Seixes of the Mikveh Israel Synagogue opposed this match, because according to Jewish law a Cohen, as a descendant of the priestly caste, is forbidden to marry a widow (Leviticus 21:14). But Jacob defiantly married Elizabeth anyway, barely escaping excommunication. It is unknown who performed the marriage, but Haym Salomon was a witness and signed their ketubah. The renowned Salomon's support would have served as a seal of approval. Nevertheless, the newlyweds soon moved to Richmond, Virginia. Returning to Philadelphia twenty-eight years later, all was forgiven and Cohen was made president of the congregation.

Why had Jacob Cohen defied Jewish law in his marriage to Elizabeth Mordecai? Love, of course, is one reason, but it's also important to remember how few Jews resided in the colonies during this time. By the end of the Revolutionary War, the Jewish population in Philadelphia amounted to fewer than five hundred, making it extremely difficult to find a mate within the faith.

Meanwhile, Moses Mordecai's son, Jacob, married Judith Myers, the daughter of a famous silversmith of that era, Myer Myers. Myers was a renowned artisan who made tea sets, candelabras and cutlery. He also created seven splendid Torah finials, two of which today are found on the Ark of the Mikveh Israel Synagogue.

5. CHRIST CHURCH CEMETERY

This historic cemetery—final resting place of Revolutionary War heroes, victims of the yellow fever epidemic of 1793 and notables like Benjamin Franklin—may be entered on Arch Street near the corner of Market Street. The burial ground is an extension of the cemetery adjoining Christ Church at Second Street and Market, where we paused earlier. The burial ground was closed to the public in the last decades of the twentieth century for restoration and then reopened in 2003. The cemetery is open daily Monday through Saturday between 10:00 a.m. and 4:00 p.m. and on Sunday from 12:00 p.m. to 4:00 p.m. It is closed in January and February and on rainy days.

The church's knowledgeable docents are ready to help locate graves and provide fascinating stories about the interred. Visitors may wander the cemetery on their own with maps provided at the entrance or join one of the hourly guided tours. And although a modest fee is charged to enter the burial ground, the staff will cheerfully point out that the Franklin grave can be quite easily seen from the street, through a convenient opening in the wall.

Graves date from the colonial era. The original wall was built in 1722, enclosing two acres. There are 4,000 plots with 1,400 gravestones. The last burial here was in 1997.

The most frequently visited grave is that of Franklin, buried prominently on the northwest corner alongside his wife, Deborah, and their children, Francis and Sarah. But before we get there, we pass a most unusual memorial—that of Major David Salisbury Franks. His marker can be found just inside the cemetery gate. Look down and find a small memorial plaque placed on the ground immediately to the right of the entrance, with an American flag next to it. But how did a Jewish man come to be laid to rest at the Christ Church Cemetery? Thereby hangs a sorry tale.

Franks was born in Philadelphia in 1740, the son of a successful merchant. His family relocated to Quebec when he was a young man. In 1775, on the eve of the American Revolution, Franks was living in Montreal and serving as parnas (president) of the Spanish Portuguese Synagogue there.

When the Continental army invaded Quebec in an attempt to wrest it from British control, Franks joined the rebellion and took up arms. He was eventually appointed paymaster of the Continental army in Quebec and apparently advanced his own funds to pay salaries of American troops.

After the Quebec campaign faltered, Franks returned to the city of his birth in July 1776 and rejoined the Continental army here. Since he had combat experience, he was quickly given the rank of major. This was the highest rank for a Jewish officer at the time. Because he spoke French, Franks was assigned as liaison officer to the Comte d'Estaing, commander of the French naval forces fighting on the American side.

Franks's misfortunes began when he was appointed aide-de-camp to General Benedict Arnold. This appointment was to mar him for life. Arnold was assigned to the strategic garrison at West Point. When Arnold tried to surrender West Point to the British and eventually went over to the British side, he was branded a traitor. Poor Franks was similarly charged with disloyalty, a case of guilt by association. But matters were made even worse because he had an uncle with the identical name, David Franks. Unlike David S. Franks, his uncle was a Tory sympathizer, whose daughter, Rebecca, once hosted a fête to honor General William Howe, the British commander in chief.

According to the American Jewish Historical Society, charges of treason were lodged against our David Franks. For what it was worth, Arnold even wrote a letter denying any complicity with Franks. The case resulted in an acquittal by George Washington himself, who had Franks reassigned to the army. But suspicions against Franks persisted. As a result, Franks requested that another military court investigate his case, with a full trial. Nothing could be found against him, and again Franks was cleared of all charges.

As a sign that the American leadership valued him, David Salisbury Franks was accepted as a member of the political-philosophical Society of Cincinnati shortly after that society was founded in 1783. Its credo was to preserve ideals and fellowship of the Revolution. It still exists today.

Also in 1783, Franks was entrusted by the State Department to carry highly classified documents to Benjamin Franklin in Paris, including the peace treaty that ended the war and recognized American independence. Not properly funded to carry out this mission, Franks reportedly subsidized the journey himself. His other mission at that time was to carry classified documents to diplomat John Jay in Madrid. Back at home, meanwhile, Jeffersonian Republicans conducted a whispering campaign, again casting doubt on Franks's loyalty, and this brought about his dismissal from the diplomatic service in 1786. He returned to the United States discredited and bankrupt. But like Haym Salomon, Franks fought

D.S. Franks burial marker located at Christ Church Cemetery. *Photograph by author.*

like a lion for his reputation and in 1789 petitioned Washington for a new appointment. Congress eventually granted him four hundred acres for all he had done for the war effort.

Franks's last position was that of assistant cashier of the Bank of the United States in Philadelphia. Franks, however, would continue to feel stigmatized for the remainder of his life, and four years later, during the great yellow fever outbreak in 1793, Franks died at age fifty-two, poor and all but forgotten. His corpse was piled onto a coroner's wagon for a quick burial in the potter's field, an area today known as Washington Square. But at the last moment, a neighbor, a member of Christ Church, recognized Franks and convinced the church that this fine citizen deserved a proper resting place. Because of the numerous hasty burials that year when four thousand lives were lost to the epidemic, it is not known exactly where Franks lies. But at least we have the little memorial in the cemetery. In addition, in October 2004 the Pennsylvania Historical and Museum Commission erected a blue and gold marker commemorating him outside the cemetery on Fifth Street, near the corner of Arch Street. Franks was suggested for such commemoration by Donald U.

Smith, executive director of the Christ Church Preservation Trust, in cooperation with the Feinstein Center of Temple University.

Moving a few yards along the wall from the Franks memorial to the northwest corner of the cemetery, we come to the resting place of one of Philadelphia's most illustrious citizens, Benjamin Franklin. Boston was his birthplace, and Boston may claim him as its own, but Franklin arrived in Philadelphia at age seventeen and made his name here.

The grave is easy to find. It's the one adorned with pennies tossed by visitors. Franklin's grave rests exactly across the street from where the coins are produced—the United States Mint. Why the pennies? Likely in honor of Ben's famous proverb: "A penny saved is a penny earned." Or maybe the pennies are dropped simply for good luck. No one knows for sure how the practice of placing pennies here began, but the church nevertheless puts the coins toward maintenance of the cemetery.

Whole libraries, it seems, have been written about this printer, publisher, scientist and statesman, so I'm going to focus on Franklin and the Jews, if only to refute the hoary rumor that he was an anti-Semite. Indeed, anyone who knows Franklin's story would recognize that such an outlandish canard contradicts all that Franklin stood for.

The anti-Semitic accusations concerning Franklin date to the Nazi era, according to Lance Sussman, rabbi of Philadelphia's suburban Congregation Keneseth Israel and a scholar of American history. Nazi propagandists believed that claiming that an iconic American figure such as Franklin hated Jews would somehow help promote and legitimize their agenda among Americans.

Just why the Nazis seized on Franklin is unclear. Possibly it was because Franklin's long career as a scientist and as a diplomat in Europe had made him the best-known early American figure among Germans. Who knows? One usually searches in vain for "logic" behind anti-Semitism. In any event, the false accusations unfortunately gained some circulation among fascist supporters in the United States. But anyone bothering to search for expressions of anti-Semitism in Franklin's voluminous writings will search in vain.

A Pennsylvania state marker commemorating D.S. Franks, commissioned in 2004. *Photograph by author.*

Franklin's grave at Christ Church Cemetery, Fifth and Arch Streets. *Photograph by author.*

When Franklin arrived in Philadelphia, he began working with a printer named Samuel Keiner, who published a book titled *Hebrew and Other Languages*. Franklin was largely self-taught, having been forced to leave school at age twelve to begin an apprenticeship in printing. Starved for books, he read all that he could get. But aside from the Bible, Keiner's book was quite possibly Franklin's first exposure to anything Jewish.

Franklin founded his own press within a short time, and this allowed him to meet all sorts of Philadelphians, among them businessman Nathan Levy, with whom he became good friends. When Franklin learned of Levy's urgent need to bury his young child, Franklin helped him procure land for what would become the city's first Jewish cemetery and then helped him survey it. In 1782, Franklin also pledged £5—approximately $800 in today's dollars—in support of a synagogue for "the people of the Hebrew society in the city of Philadelphia." This was the Mikveh Israel Synagogue. The signed pledge is today in the collection of the National Museum of American Jewish History. Franklin moreover suggested selling lottery tickets to raise funds to build the synagogue. This was based on the success of Franklin's fundraising scheme for the Christ Church steeple. Years later, Franklin also personally wrote Levy's obituary in his newspaper.

Franklin's *Pennsylvania Gazette* also prominently reported and decried anti-Semitic attacks occurring in Germany. In 1737, Franklin noted in the *Gazette* that "the Jews were acquainted with several arts and sciences long e're the Romans became a people, or the Greeks were known among nations." Added Franklin, "If the Greeks had been acquainted with the Songs of Moses, or the Romans had known of the Odes of David, they would never had spoken against the Jews with such contempt."

The fact was that Franklin was quick to defend any oppressed community. His famous defiant act to save Indians from a lynch mob, for example, would surely have resonated among the small local Jewish community, a group all too familiar with European pogroms. A gang of vigilantes known as "the Paxton Boys" was in pursuit of "Redskins" in retaliation for the killing of a white man. The Indians had sought refuge in Philadelphia, which since the days of William Penn had been known for its coexistence with Indians.

Franklin personally confronted the vigilantes as they entered the city, whooping and bent on murdering any Indian they could find. Franklin persuaded them to petition the authorities with their grievances, and afterward the gang dispersed. That's the kind of man Ben Franklin was.

Among the many other colonial notables buried in the Christ Church Cemetery is John Dunlap. He is buried in Section A, near the tree on the right-hand side as you enter the grounds. His history includes an amusing Jewish anecdote. Dunlap was the printer who published the first broadsides of the Declaration of Independence. One is located in the American Philosophical Society building in the Independence Hall courtyard at Fifth and Chestnut Streets. It can be viewed upon request. Another, more accessible one is found within the same courtyard at Sixth and Chestnut Streets in the west wing of Independence Hall. But Independence Hall does not have the Yiddish version.

How's that? Well, a Jew named Jonas Phillips had a shop near Dunlap's printing office on Market Street. The enthusiastic Phillips rushed to put one of the first purchased broadsides of the Declaration of Independence in the mail to a friend in Amsterdam, along with a translation in Yiddish. Phillips decided to post it by way of the Caribbean island of St. Eustatius in order to avoid the British naval blockade. The letter was nonetheless intercepted by the British, who believed that the Yiddish was a code and sent it on to London, where it was filed away in the Public Record Office.

The Dunlap broadside was printed on July 4, 1776, and read out in public four days later. Today only twenty-six of the original two hundred hastily printed broadsides, the ones signed by John Hancock and Charles Thompson, are known to exist. Amazingly, one broadside was found recently in a flea market hidden behind a framed painting. Norman Lear, the noted Jewish TV writer-producer and political activist, eventually bought the broadside for more than $8 million and displayed it around the country, ending its journey on July 4, 2004, in Philadelphia.

But for now, our walking tour takes us south a half-block on Fifth Street. Look for the sculpture of *Religious Justice*. Just to the left is the historic Mikveh Israel Synagogue.

6. MIKVEH ISRAEL SYNAGOGUE

The synagogue is the third oldest in America. The oldest is Shearith Israel, established in 1729 in New York; the second oldest is the Touro Synagogue, dedicated in Newport, Rhode Island, in 1765. Mikveh Israel was established in 1770 and like the other two conducts services according to the Spanish-Portuguese minhag (custom). Its full name is Kahal Kadosh Mikveh Israel (the Holy Congregation of the Hope of Israel).

The present synagogue is the congregation's fourth site and fifth building. (The 1782 building and the 1825 building stood on the same lot.) The first could seat only two hundred, and when it became inadequate, it was razed to build a larger one. Mikveh Israel's last move was in 1976, leaving the building it had occupied since 1906 at Broad Street near Girard Avenue. America's Bicentennial brought major changes to the historic section of Philadelphia, including a new visitor's center, a new Liberty Bell Pavilion and new Independence Mall landscaping. The synagogue and its museum were invited to be part of the new design. It is situated on the walkway between Fourth and Fifth Streets and between Market and Arch Streets. It is the only religious institution on the mall.

The earlier synagogues no longer exist, which is regrettable, because some were designed by leading architects of their day and were splendid to behold. But portions of those buildings had to be sold off to finance subsequent ones. The second building on Cherry Alley, for example, was completed in 1825. It was designed by William Strictland in an Egyptian Revival style inspired by recent exciting finds in pyramid excavations in Egypt. Strictland's stunning architecture can be seen elsewhere in the historic area, such as the Second Bank, now our National Portrait Gallery on Chestnut Street near Fifth Street.

Haym Salomon and Miriam and Michael Gratz were the main contributors to the construction of that building. Cherished donations were made by non-Jews, as well, such as Benjamin Franklin, Benjamin Rush and Christ Church. These contributions, so welcoming to the small Jewish community, proved the integration and warm acceptance they were receiving with their neighbors.

Hand-carved Elijah Chair, Mikveh Israel Synagogue. *Photograph by author.*

Mikveh Israel's third building was designed by John McArthur in 1859, on Seventh Street, north of Arch Street. He also designed Philadelphia's grandiose City Hall—still the largest city hall in the United States. The current synagogue was to be designed by another great Philadelphia architect, Louis I. Kahn. Kahn was known to have uncompromising standards—too uncompromising, as it turned out, for the congregation. Kahn envisioned a cluster of buildings, with a sanctuary, school and museum in separate enclosures. If you are curious about that design, New York's Museum of Modern Art has his charcoal drawings done in 1963–64 housed in its permanent collection. The congregation's budget, however, would not allow for this complicated concept, and Kahn would not modify it. Yet some of Kahn's touches, such as the long narrow windows near the ceiling line providing indirect lighting, were retained. Kahn's blueprints also suggested a castle motif, with modified turrets and Roman arches, but these elements were not retained.

A few items in the synagogue are artifacts from the earlier Mikveh Israel buildings. The beautifully hand-carved Chair of Elijah had been donated by Moses Lopez in 1816 in honor of his acceptance as a congregation member. (At that time membership followed a three-year "trial period.") An Elijah Chair is almost always found in Sephardic synagogues. Traditionally, the chair is used by the sandak (godfather) during the Brit Milah (circumcision) ceremony. This one, bearing the sign of the high priest's blessing, also held the ritual washing vessel used by the rabbi during services. The passage carved in Hebrew on the chair is from Numbers 6:23: "You shall be aware of the People of Israel and bless them." The carver ran out of space for the

Top: Ark of the Mikveh Israel Synagogue displaying nineteen Torah scrolls and an Esther scroll. *Photograph by author.*

Bottom: Detail of the silver rimonim (pomegranate) finials adorning the Torah scrolls at the Mikveh Israel Synagogue. *Photograph by author.*

full passage and had to carve the last word—"l'hem"—on the chair's right side. The chair's patina glaze gives the appearance of bronze, but the chair is actually wooden.

The reading table, alternately called a shulchan, tebah or bimah, was saved from the third building. It is made of Italian marble. The Torah collection today numbers nineteen scrolls. There are twenty slots in the aron kodesh (Holy Ark), and the last slot holds a megillah (Book of Esther, read at Purim). Two Torah scrolls have the precious finials, scroll handle decorations, fashioned like pomegranates (rimonim) and crafted by the famous colonial silversmith Myer Myers, who made only seven pairs of these finials in his lifetime. Others can be found in the Shearith Israel Synagogue in New York and in the Touro Synagogue in Newport. Mikveh Israel's finials were purchased by Haym Salomon in 1782 to commemorate the completion of the first building.

Now to discuss the "inner beauty" of Mikveh Israel Synagogue—by that I mean the outstanding leaders who contributed to the personality of the building and the Jewish community of the city of Philadelphia. Three in particular immediately come to mind.

The congregation's first leader was Hazan Gershom Mendes Seixes, who arrived "on loan" from New York's Shearith Israel Congregation. There was not a single ordained rabbi in this early colonial period, as no rabbi was yet prepared to abandon his congregation or yeshiva for the wilderness of the New World. Seixes' converso parents arrived in America fleeing Portuguese persecution, and their son became the first native-born head of a Jewish congregation in the colonies. Remarkably, he began serving the New York congregation at the age of twenty-three. He would have remained there, but when the British captured New York between 1775 and 1783, the Shearith Israel members dispersed, and Seixes came to Philadelphia until New York was returned to the colonists.

While in Philadelphia, Seixes was instrumental in getting the young synagogue off the ground. He arrived with a borrowed Torah scroll and quickly set about creating a religious center at which Jewish newcomers could gather, pray, educate their children and acclimate in the New Land. This last service was especially crucial, as there were only about 2,500 Jews in all of the colonies at the time, mainly dispersed in five coastal cities. Approximately 500 of them were living in Philadelphia.

Gershom Mendes Seixes, who had twenty-six children, lived between 1746 and 1816. Known as the "Rabbi of the Revolution," he introduced the Torah discussions (d'varim) in English. During services, he often spoke out in support of the American Revolution. He was invited to attend George Washington's second inauguration. One of his brothers was an officer in the Continental army.

Well educated both in Jewish and secular subjects, the cantor managed to create a distinctly American Jewish congregation. His work entailed leadership, education of the children, interpretation of Jewish law, supervision of kashrut and officiating at marriages and funerals. Attendance at services was recorded, and congregation members were fined if caught working on Shabbat. This last point was problematic, as the Jews were fined by the city for working on Sunday. The matter was eventually sorted out, but it was one of the many hurdles Jews had to face in their newly chosen home.

Shortly after the War of Independence, Seixes returned to New York. Another significant leader soon followed: Isaac Leeser.

Leeser had arrived in Richmond, Virginia, from Prussia in 1823 at age seventeen, well educated in Talmud and in secular subjects. He spoke English, Latin, German and Hebrew. In 1829, he was invited to serve as leader of Congregation Mikveh Israel, which he did until 1850. Despite opposition from many congregants, he began to integrate English into the services. He offered Torah drashim (sermons delivered after the Torah is returned to the Ark) in English. These sermons lasted between thirty and forty minutes. As Rabbi Lance Sussman, author of a monograph on Leeser, explained, the men would leave before the sermons began, and the women would stay. And the men sulked at home, waiting to be served their Shabbat meal.

Isaac Leeser was the father of Conservative Judaism. He introduced English prayers along with Hebrew ones. This was radical for the time in the United States. Leeser founded America's first Jewish religious school, America's first Jewish theological seminary, Maimonides College and the Jewish Publication Society—all in Philadelphia. He translated both the Bible and the prayer book into English and founded and edited a highly influential Jewish newspaper, the *Occident*. All of these activities helped shape the character of American Jewry for generations to come.

Isaac Leeser was known as the most prolific Jewish religious writer of his day. His first sermon was delivered in June 1830. He would publish over 250, many appearing in his book *Discourses in the Jewish Religion*. Yet he could barely support himself and could not broker either a raise in salary or a tenured position at Mikveh Israel. He left somewhat bitter. His next position as leader was at Congregation Beth-El-Emeth in Philadelphia, beginning in 1857 and lasting until his death in 1868.

Shortly after Leeser's withdrawal from Mikveh Israel Synagogue, he was replaced by Sabato Morais. Morais's family came from Portugal, but their son was born in America. Morais was outspoken in his condemnation of slavery. He, along with a few others, was also instrumental in establishing the Jewish Theological Seminary in New York in 1886. He died in Philadelphia in 1897.

Mikveh Israel is currently led by Rabbi Albert Gabbai, a native of Egypt. Visitors are welcome to attend services. Women are seated separately but not hidden behind a divider, and services are still in the Spanish tradition, even though the majority of the members today are Ashkenazim.

A question I am invariably asked by tour groups is the meaning of "mikveh." As noted earlier, in reference to the synagogue, it means "Hope of Israel" (as you no doubt know, Israel's national anthem, "Hatikvah," means "The Hope"). However, yes, a mikveh is also a ritual bath. The Hebrew root letters are the same, as is the pronunciation. This is one of the few instances in Hebrew when apparently unrelated meanings arise from the same root.

Outside the synagogue is a striking sculpture. It is cut from a single block of Vermont granite, which resembles Jerusalem stone, into four pillars. The sculpture is by Israeli artist Buky Schwartz and memorializes Yonatan Netanyahu, who led the Israeli rescue of hostages from the Air France plane that was hijacked to Uganda in 1976. Netanyahu was the only soldier slain in the operation. The sculpture was funded by local art patrons Muriel and Philip Berman and by classmates of Yonatan Netanyahu, who, along with

Religious Liberty, commissioned in 1876 by B'nai B'rith for the Centennial World Fair Exhibition and later moved to Mikveh Israel during the Bicentennial celebration in Independence National Park in 1976. It was moved again, to the National Museum of American Jewish History, in 2010. Sculpture by Sir Moses Ezekiel. *Photograph by author.*

his brother, the future Israeli prime minister Benjamin Netanyahu, attended Philadelphia's suburban Cheltenham High School while their father was a visiting professor here.

I remember the rescue operation well, for I was among the hundreds of thousands of Israelis who converged on Tel Aviv's Ben Gurion Airport to welcome home the freed hostages. This was on July 4, 1976, a day that will forever be for me "Yom Entebbe," as well as the U.S. Bicentennial Independence Day.

Religious Liberty is the other sculpture standing by the synagogue on the Fifth Street side. It was commissioned by the B'nai B'rith and created by Sir Moses Jacob Ezekiel for the nation's centennial celebration. Originally, it stood in Philadelphia's Fairmont Park but was moved to this location in 1985. It announced the synagogue's National Museum of American Jewish History, which is slated to open in late 2010 in its new location nearby at Fifth and Market Streets.

Let's now walk south along Fifth to Market and learn more about the vastly expanded National Museum of American Jewish History.

7. The National Museum of American Jewish History

Of the fifty-two Jewish museums in the United States, Philadelphia's National Museum of American Jewish History is the only one devoted to chronicling the entire 350-year history of Jews in this country.

The NMAJH was established as part of the Mikveh Israel Synagogue when the congregation moved to the Independence Mall during America's Bicentennial celebration in 1976. The museum was built around Mikveh Israel artifacts, such as a letter from President Washington thanking the congregation for its good wishes after his inauguration, and other possessions of the congregation from the colonial period through to the twentieth century. But soon enough, the permanent collection and its special exhibitions were leaving the museum cramped for space.

Now the NMAJH is getting its own very sizeable building. Mikveh Israel will gain badly needed space. Until now, for example, its entrance gallery was the only space for public events like receptions and for post-Shabbat service luncheons, which required hastily setting up wall-to-wall tables.

The new museum, happily, is just a few minutes' walk from the synagogue and still in a prestigious place on Independence Mall. It's at the corner of Fifth and Market Streets, not far from the Liberty Bell Pavilion. Thus the museum is at the heart of the action. The bell receives over 2 million visitors a year, and Independence Hall, just another few minutes away, receives 4 million visitors. The NMAJH hopes to have 225,000 visitors annually.

The new premises are scheduled to open in November 2010. Philanthropist Sidney Kimmel, the twenty-first-century Medici

The National Museum of American Jewish History. *National Museum of American Jewish History*

of Philadelphia culture, jointly started the NMAJH by pledging $25 million toward its construction. Kimmel had already given a large enough sum to have the city's Kimmel Center for Performing Arts named after him, as well as giving millions to area Jewish schools that might have closed without his contributions. Kimmel, who owns Jones Apparel NY, says he discovered his Jewishness at age seventy-three, when he celebrated his bar mitzvah.

Additional funds for the NMAJH came from Ed Snider, Comcast-Spectacor, the Dell Foundation and from donors who each contributed over $1 million. The state of Pennsylvania contributed $22 million, and the City gave $1 million. To date, 80 percent of the funding is donations outside the state. As of June 2009, $100 of a $150 million goal had been reached. Money is going to building and development costs, as well as an endowment.

The museum's CEO and president is Dr. Michael Rosenzweig, assisted by a staff of distinguished scholars like Jonathan Sarna, professor of American Jewish History at Brandeis University. The mission statement of the educational programs and experiences that preserve, explore, and celebrate the history of the Jews in America."

The museum hopes to attract both Jewish and non-Jewish visitors. It plans on hosting school groups and developing a community outreach program. Its view is that the Jewish immigration story could be the story of any ethnic group finding its place in America.

The permanent collection will occupy much of the five-story glass building, which was designed by James Polshek, architect of the William Jefferson Clinton Library in Little Rock, Arkansas, and the Rose Center for Earth and Space in Manhattan. The building's transparency, the architect says, is to suggest that American Jewish life deserves full exposure. Passersby on the street will be able to look right through the building, and visitors inside will be able to look out and see the great landmarks of America's founding.

Three stories will feature works from the permanent collection, and one story will have rotating exhibits. Elsewhere will be a research department, an archive, an auditorium and a café. An

Shochet's knife and sheath. *National Museum of American Jewish History.*

entrance gallery will contain "The Hall of Fame" honoring prominent American Jews like composers Irving Berlin, Aaron Copland and Leonard Bernstein, writers like Isaac Bashevis Singer, Arthur Miller and Saul Bellow and statesmen, Supreme Court justices and Nobel Prize winners. An eight-foot flame will be incorporated in the atrium.

In all, the museum has 100,000 square feet for displaying the more than twenty-five thousand artifacts in its collection. Items range from a shochet knife (for ritual slaughtering of animals) with an American flag painted on its sheath to Torah bells fashioned by colonial silversmith Myer Myers; also included are a promissory note written by Benjamin Franklin to Mikveh Israel Synagogue and a copy of "A Prayer for the Medina," composed by the Richmond congregation in 1789 honoring the adoption of the U.S. Constitution.

You may learn more about the museum's collection and about the past twenty exhibitions at Mikveh Israel by checking out the museum's website, www.nmajh.org, as well as follow progress toward completion of the new premises.

8. THE LIBERTY BELL

Cross Market Street and you can't miss the Liberty Bell Pavilion on Independence Mall. In May and June, the lines can wrap around the side of the long building (all those school groups!), and the wait to enter can take over an hour. As at Independence Hall, one must pass a security check. Unlike at Independence Hall, however, no prearranged ticket is required. National Park rangers relate a short history of the bell, and intriguing historical artifacts are displayed on the way to the bell chamber. There's also a film and reading material in numerous languages (including Hebrew). Photography is allowed. The bell chamber is open daily, 9:00 a.m. to 5:00 p.m. In the evening hours, recordings of the bell's history can be heard near the exterior window panel immediately outside the chamber on the mall side by selecting your language and activating the switch.

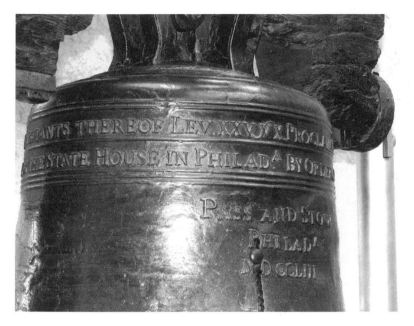

The Liberty Bell, with the passage from Leviticus. *Photograph by author.*

The Pennsylvania State House Bell, as it was originally known, was commissioned in 1751 to hang in the tower of the Pennsylvania State House to commemorate the fiftieth anniversary of William Penn's "Charter of Privileges." Penn's charter, Pennsylvania's original constitution, speaks of rights and freedoms valued by people everywhere. These included religious freedom, the rights of the Indians and inclusion of the citizens to create laws; these were very liberal and forward-thinking for the time.

Isaac Norris, a Quaker and speaker of the Pennsylvania Assembly, was in charge of commissioning the bell. Norris, who knew his Hebrew Bible, chose for the bell's inscription a phrase from Leviticus 25:10: "Proclaim liberty throughout all the land unto all the inhabitants thereof." The word for liberty in Hebrew is *dror*, meaning release. As the Lord says, "You shall hallow the 50th year. You shall proclaim release throughout the land for all its inhabitants. It shall be a jubilee for you." It was the perfect passage to celebrate the jubilee year of Penn's establishment of the Pennsylvania Commonwealth.

Independence Hall bell tower, the original home of the Liberty Bell. *Photograph by author.*

The bell arrived from the Whitechapel Foundry in London in 1752. It was the first bell that the foundry cast. The bell, which weighs slightly over a ton (2,080 pounds), was transported on a ship named the *Myrtilla*, one of many owned by the fleet partners David Franks and Nathan Levy. It is believed to have arrived with an undetected hairline crack that would spread each time the bell was struck.

Whitechapel insisted that the bell was sent flawless. Maybe. But it would have been impractical to return it. All that's known is that the crack began to widen with each clang of the clapper. Within a year, the bell had developed a dissonant hum. This led to it being recast by a local foundry with more experience casting bells. That foundry's name is cast on the bell Pass and Stow. They hoped that by adding a higher copper content in ratio to the tin and the other bronze alloys (traces of arsenic, gold and silver) the bell it would be less brittle. But apparently the formula was still not right.

When the British occupied the city in September 1777, the bell, crack and all, was secretly rushed sixty miles north to Allentown, Pennsylvania, and hidden there, lest it be melted down by the Redcoats and cast into cannonballs. In May 1778, shortly after Washington's successful campaign from Valley Forge and the British retreat from Philadelphia, the bell was returned home.

The bell was rung on July 8, 1776, summoning citizens to hear the first public reading of the Declaration of Independence by Colonel John Nixon in the courtyard of Independence Hall. With the Declaration of Independence, the colonies became the United States.

The bell was also sounded to inform congressmen and senators when to go to work (remember, Philadelphia was our nation's capital from 1790 to 1800) and then each time a resident of Philadelphia succumbed to yellow fever. That repeated tolling depressed the public so much that it was finally discontinued.

Often a National Park ranger will state that the bell cracked simply because it was old. Yet this bell is still comparatively young. Bells can last for many centuries. In any event, our bell is believed to have been struck for the last time in 1846 to commemorate George

Washington's birthday. But other stories of the bell's final clang abound. No one knows for certain.

People are always surprised to see the width of the crack. But what they see is not really the flaw in the bell. This space was created by drilling around the crack in an attempt to prevent the flaw from spreading. Unfortunately, a new crack began to spread to the bell's crown above the stopgap drilling, making it virtually impossible to repair.

It was therefore replaced by another bell, and the original, which you see before you, sat in the Independence Hall courtyard until the Bicentennial year of 1976, when it was transferred to an enclosed pavilion on the mall, directly across the street from Independence Hall. The final move occurred in 2003, when it was conveyed a few feet to its present site. To celebrate that move, the park staff served up bell-shaped pancakes to the crowd gathered to watch the short but historic relocation.

How the bell cracked is the most common question tourists ask. The second almost always is: "Is this the real bell?" It is, and I confess that each time I enter the bell chamber I get goose bumps. It is a thrilling sight to behold. And really, the story of the bell is what makes it significant—not the crack. This silent bell draws more people together than any working bell. Park statistics state that the Bell Center attracts over two million visitors annually from all over the world.

The power of this bell to speak to freedom-loving people was recognized by President Lincoln, who immediately after the Civil War ordered the bell to be conveyed by train around the nation. The idea was to bring together the war-torn country by reminding all Americans, north and south, of their common heritage.

You'll note that so far I haven't often used the name "Liberty Bell." That's because it didn't get that name until long after it was commissioned as the Pennsylvania State House Bell. First, an image of the bell adorned a pamphlet printed by the Friends of Freedom in Boston, an abolitionist movement originating in 1839. Then in 1848, in Seneca Falls, New York, Elizabeth Cady Stanton began using the same image in the literature promoting women's right to vote. These and other rights groups referred to the symbol as the Liberty Bell, and eventually the Pennsylvania State House Bell became universally known as the Liberty Bell.

The Liberty Bell's symbolic power has hardly been eclipsed. Nelson Mandela made a pilgrimage to the bell when apartheid ended in South Africa. West German chancellor Willy Brandt paid a similar visit after the Berlin Wall was torn down. So don't be surprised if during your visit Tibetan monks are on the scene praying for greater freedom for their country, or if some other group is demonstrating to make known its cause. In addition, many facsimiles of the bell are displayed throughout the world, including one in Jerusalem's Gan HaPa'amon (Bell Park).

Our last stop, not often included in my three-hour walking tour, is six blocks away. We leave the main historic area and head toward the Society Hill neighborhood. But don't fret, there is no hill. The walk is all level, and the eighteenth-century homes along the way make for a pleasant stroll

You will be exiting the Bell Pavilion at Sixth and Chestnut Streets. Continue south on Sixth Street, passing Walnut, and keep walking the short distance until Spruce Street. Turn right on Spruce and head west to Ninth Street. There on the right side you will find the Mikveh Israel Cemetery. If it is a really hot day, however, hop on a bus on Spruce Street going west and request the Pennsylvania Hospital bus stop.

9. MIKVEH ISRAEL CEMETERY

Like the Old City, which we've just been visiting, Society Hill is part of Philadelphia's earliest areas of settlement. It is pleasant to walk the streets here, now gentrified and becoming more exclusive; Society Hill is even occasionally referred to as New York City's sixth borough. Yet this is also the location of the venerable Mikveh Israel Cemetery, on Spruce Street between Eighth and Ninth Streets and across from the historic Pennsylvania Hospital. Its last burial took place in 1958. Two years after that it was designated a national shrine by Congress and is now considered part of Independence National Historic Park.

Mikveh Israel Cemetery gate. *Photograph by author.*

The cemetery is often locked, but from mid-June to mid-August the gates are open on Sunday and on Tuesday through Friday, from 10:00 a.m. to 3:00 p.m. (It is, however, closed on rainy days.) Groups are welcome at other times, but such visits must be arranged in advance by calling the Mikveh Israel Synagogue office at 215-922-5446. In addition, the gates are opened for Yizkor (memorial) services between Rosh Hashanah and Yom Kippur and on the anniversary of Haym Salomon's death in January.

This cemetery's previous location, purchased from colony proprietor Thomas Penn, was used for only two years in 1738. It was a small, dusty field on the outskirts of town. That was where Nathan Levy buried his young child. Today it's the site of the Walnut Street Theatre, the oldest theatre in America. When a larger and more central cemetery was needed in anticipation of the establishment of Mikveh Israel Synagogue and a growing Jewish population, the new burial ground was secured at this site in 1740. Benjamin Franklin himself helped to broker the deal and survey the land and suggested a lottery to help finance the sale. Levy reinterred his child here.

This graveyard is one of the earliest Jewish cemeteries in the nation, and the Mikveh Israel Synagogue dates its founding from establishment of the cemetery. The original area measured 30 square feet. More land measuring 30 feet wide and 60 feet long was offered to Levy in 1752 to adjoin the space. In 1765, Mathias Bush purchased yet more land from John Penn. This area measures 60 feet long and 127 feet wide.

Look through the iron gate, and the first grave marker is that of Haym Salomon. Salomon was a pillar of the Mikveh Israel Synagogue, but when he was buried here his family lacked enough funds for a tombstone. As the years passed, then, his actual burial spot was forgotten. Why this should have happened is puzzling, because the caretakers were known to keep impeccable records, and Salomon was a major contributor to the 1782 synagogue. In an attempt to finally set things right, a marble tablet was placed on the east wall, installed by his great-grandson, William Salomon.

Mikveh Israel Cemetery. *Photograph by author.*

Look down to notice the granite memorial set inside the gate with funds provided by Haym Salomon Lodge 663 of the Brith Shalom fraternal organization.

By contrast, the plot of Nathan Levy, the instigator of the Jewish burial ground, is prominently located smack in the center of the cemetery, next to the graveyard's only tree. Levy died in 1753.

In 1886, the cemetery was declared filled. But room was, in fact, found for three more Mikveh Israel congregants. Josephine Etting had bought her grave fifty years before her demise, and she was duly buried here in 1913. Fanny Polano Elmaleh, the wife of congregation leader Reverend Leon Elmaleh, was buried here in 1966, and her husband was laid to rest here in 1972. Three earlier Mikveh Israel rabbis are buried here, but the noted Rabbi Isaac Lesser is not among them—perhaps, as we learned earlier, due to his untimely and bitter departure from his pulpit. Leeser's brother, Jacob, however, lies here. Twenty-one Revolutionary War soldiers and scores of veterans of the War of 1812 are here as well.

Unusual for any Jewish cemetery of that time, the esteemed Gratz family has a sixty-foot parcel of land next to the plots of patriarch Michael and matriarch Miriam Gratz. Almost all of their twelve children and the children's families are buried together here. In all, there are twenty-five conterminous burial plots allocated for the Gratz family, almost a memorial park unto itself. Even the larger New York Jewish community did not permit so much space to be allotted at that time to one family. But in 1813, after the deaths of both parents, Mikveh Israel decided that the much-loved Gratz family, all pillars of the community, deserved no less. Considering that the synagogue already had one hundred members at the end of the Revolutionary War, the amount of land set aside for the Gratzes was considerable.

Of Michael and Miriam's five daughters and seven sons, Rebecca Gratz (1781–1869) is best known today. By all accounts, she was beautiful, brilliant and well read. Rebecca was the first Jewish woman in the colonies to attend college—Franklin College, as it was known then (Franklin and Marshall College today), in Lancaster, Pennsylvania. Even though Mama Gratz's family lived in Lancaster, allowing Rebecca to study and board far from home in an almost all-male college indicated her parents' enlightenment—and their trust. Indeed, when Rebecca fell in love with a gentile named Samuel Ewing, she ended the relationship out of religious conviction and never married. Instead, she dedicated her life to establishing many charities and caring for her aging parents.

Ewing, incidentally, did eventually marry but confessed to his wife that Rebecca would always be his great love. When he died at thirty-nine, Rebecca surprised the other mourners by walking over to the open coffin, placing three white roses and a miniature of herself on Ewing's chest and silently retreating.

Rebecca Gratz eventually befriended the writer Washington Irving, and Irving described her to Sir Walter Scott, who reportedly modeled the virtuous Rebecca in his novel *Ivanhoe* after her. Perhaps he had become enthralled with the story of Rebecca Gratz's thwarted romance. For her part, Rebecca Gratz was something of a writer herself, and her voluminous letters allow us an invaluable description of life and times in the nineteenth century.

Her beauty inspired artists, as well. Notable portraitists of the time, including Gilbert Stuart and Thomas Sully, painted her. Outstanding portraits of Rebecca, her equally alluring sister Rachel and their father Michael Gratz may be seen in the nearby Rosenbach Library and Museum (see chapter 2 in part I). Incidentally, Rachel's husband, Solomon Etting, was among the earliest of the colonial population to oppose slavery. This couple is buried in Baltimore.

Other Gratz family members buried in the Mikveh Israel Cemetery include Simon and Bernard, successful merchants and two of the founders of the Pennsylvania Academy of Fine Arts, and Jacob, an early manager of the Jewish Publication Society. Bernard was a "pioneer" of the family who traveled as far as Pittsburgh and beyond selling merchandise. He was known to have requested a Haggadah sent to him across the Allegheny Mountains so that he could celebrate Passover when he was away from family and friends. There also is Hyman Gratz, who along with Isaac Leeser and Rebecca Gratz established a trust fund for Gratz College, founded in 1895 as a college of Jewish studies.

Pennsylvania Hospital, with statue of William Penn located by the original entrance. *Photo by the author.*

The Mikveh Israel Cemetery contains 371 identified graves. One unmarked grave is believed to be the final resting place for an African American servant of the Marks family. This servant reportedly observed all the Jewish holidays along with the family and prepared meals according to the strictest laws of kashrut. Marks petitioned the Mikveh Israel congregation for permission to bury her in the cemetery. Despite a letter written in support of this request by Rebecca Gratz, the synagogue refused. Nevertheless, Marks is alleged to have scaled the walls and buried the servant at night, near the gate. According to the custom of the time, Jews of dubious origin, gentiles married to Jews and suicides were permitted burial around the burial ground perimeter but not in the cemetery proper.

In the Revolutionary War period, a wall was erected around the cemetery when locals were found using the open space as a firing range. This practice disturbed Nathan Levy so much that he posted a sign and offered a reward to anyone who caught these disrespectful gun-toters in the act. Later on, the occupying Redcoats were known to execute deserters inside the burial ground.

The Mikveh Israel Synagogue received full title to the cemetery in 1828, and later the congregation was permitted to sell off some land to raise money for a new house of worship. An eastern portion of the cemetery grounds was sold to the Pennsylvania Hospital, and a western section was sold to the Society of Friends. In 1956, the cemetery was made a national shrine by an act of Congress, signed by President Dwight Eisenhower. In 1971, it was placed on the National Register of Historic Places, along with Christ Church and Philadelphia's Saints Peter and Paul Cathedral. In 1975, in anticipation of the Bicentennial celebration, the Colonial Philadelphia Historical Society volunteered to maintain and preserve the cemetery. Five years later, a trust was established for its perpetual maintenance as a Historic Independence Mall National Shrine.

This ends the walking tour. A stroll west on leafy Pine Street will take you to the portion of Broad Street called the Avenue of the Arts, indicated by the "Double A" lampposts. Here we return to the twenty-first century. Among the theatres and art centers on the avenue is the splendid new Kimmel Center for the Performing Arts at Broad and Pine. Philadelphia's venerable YM&WHA is located just across the street from the Kimmel Center.

Part III

APPENDIX

I t has been a while since Philadelphia's Jewish population resided in a few select neighborhoods. Today the population is distributed over a five-county area. These areas include City Center; the City Line Avenue neighborhoods of Lower Merion, Wynnefield and Overbrook Park; Main Line; the northern suburbs of Cheltenham Township (particularly Elkins Park and Melrose Park) and Upper Moreland Township; and Northeast Philadelphia. I include here only synagogues within Philadelphia. The following information was compiled by the Jewish Federation of Greater Philadelphia.

SYNAGOGUES

Conservative

Society Hill Synagogue
418 Spruce Street, Philadelphia, PA, 19106 (215-922-6599)

Temple Menorah/Keneseth Chai
4301 Tyson Avenue, Philadelphia, PA, 19135 (215-624-9600)

YPC Shari Eli
728 West Moyamensing Avenue, Philadelphia, PA, 19148 (215-339-9897)

Conservative, United Synagogue of Conservative Judaism

Congregation Melrose B'nai Israel Emanu-El
133 West Cheltenham Avenue, Cheltenham, PA, 19012 (215-635-4649)

Congregations of Ner Zedek
7520 Bustleton Avenue, Philadelphia, PA, 19152 (215-728-1155)

Germantown Jewish Centre
400 West Ellet Street, Philadelphia, PA, 19119 (215-844-1507)

Temple Adath Israel of Main Line
250 North Highland Avenue, Merion Station, PA, 19066 (610-934-1919)

Temple Beth-Zion-Beth Israel
300 South Eighteenth Street, Philadelphia, PA, 19103 (215-735-5148)

Orthodox

Beit Harambam Congregation (Sephardic)
9981 Veree Road, Philadelphia, PA, 19115 (215-677-9675)

Beth Solomon Kollel and Community Center
198 Tomlinson Road, Philadelphia, PA, 19116 (215-671-1981)

Congregation Ahavas Torah
1425 Rhawn Street, Philadelphia, PA, 19111 (215-725-3610)

Congregation B'nai Abraham
527 Lombard Street, Philadelphia, PA, 19147 (215-328-2100)

Congregation B'nai Israel/Ohev Zedek
8201 Castor Avenue, Philadelphia, PA, 19152 (215-742-0400)

Congregation B'nai Jacob
7926 Algon Avenue, Philadelphia, PA, 19111 (215-725-5182)

Congregation Mikveh Israel (Sephardic)
44 North Fourth Street, Philadelphia, PA, 19106 (215-922-5446)

Congregation Shivtei Yeshuron-Ezras Israel
2015 South Fourth Street, Philadelphia, PA, 19148 (215-704-7110)

Mekor Habracha/Center City Synagogue
127 South Twenty-second Street, Philadelphia, PA, 19103 (215-525-4246)

Raim Ahuvim
5854 Drexel Road, Philadelphia, PA, 19131 (215-878-8477)

Vilna Congregation
509 Pine Street, Philadelphia, PA, 19106 (215-574-9280)

Reconstructionist

Congregation Mishkan Shalom
4101 Freeland Avenue, Philadelphia, PA, 19128 (215-508-0226)

Leyv Ha-Ir/The Ethical Society
1906 South Rittenhouse Square, Philadelphia, PA, 19129 (215-629-1995)

Reform, Union for Reform Judaism

Congregation Beth Ahavah at Congregation Rodeph Shalom
615 North Broad Street, Philadelphia, PA, 19123; a gay and lesbian
  congregation (215-923-2003)

Congregation Rodeph Shalom
615 North Broad Street, Philadelphia, PA, 19123 (215-627-6747)

Traditional

Adath Zion Congregation
1138 Wellington Street, Philadelphia, PA, 19111 (215-742-8500)

Chabad Lubavitch Center, Regional Headquarters
7622 Castor Avenue, Philadelphia, PA, 19152 (215-725-2030)

Congregation Kesher Israel
412 Lombard Street, Philadelphia, PA, 19147 (215-922-1776)

Congregation Shaare Shamayim
9768 Verree Road, Philadelphia, PA, 19115 (215-677-1600)

Temple Beth Ami
9201 Old Bustleton Avenue, Philadelphia, PA, 19115 (215-673-
  2511)

DINING

For the most part, the restaurants listed here are in the Center
City area. Many are near the walking tour route. Several other
Jewish-style eateries are some distance from the Center City area
or in the suburbs. They are not included in this list, except for
Koch's Deli, near the University of Pennsylvania campus, and
Max and David's, near the two big synagogues in the suburb

The Famous Deli in South Philadelphia. *Photograph by author.*

of Elkins Park listed in part I of the appendix. Most of the restaurants serve "Jewish style," but a few are certified kosher, and I have indicated these.

Centennial Café

Ohio House, Belmont Avenue, in Fairmount Park, in a historical 1876 Ohio stone house remaining from the Centennial World Fair. Owner/Chef David Groverman makes fantastic smoked brisket sandwiches. Deli style found very near the newly relocated Please Touch Museum, which the entire family will love seeing (215-877-3055)

Famous Fourth Street Deli

700 Fourth Street.
Philly's most popular Jewish-style deli (215-922-3274)

Hershel's East Side Deli
Reading Terminal Market, Twelfth and Arch Streets
Long lines attest to great pastrami, corned beef and Reubens (215-922-6220)

Honey's Sit n'Eat
800 North Fourth Street, in Northern Liberties, features Jewish Southern style. Zagat Guide recommends the Reuben sandwich (215-925-1150)

Kibitz in the City
703 Chestnut Street, Washington Square East. Deli located near Independence Hall (215-928-1447)

Koch's Deli
4309 Locust Street, near UPenn campus. Closed Wednesdays (215-222-8662)

Maccabeam
128 South Twelfth Street, Israeli and Middle Eastern food (215-922 5922)

Mama's Vegetarian
18 South Twentieth Street. Closed Friday afternoons and Saturdays. Kosher (215-751-0477)

Maoz Vegetarian Restaurant
248 South Street. Open daily (215-625-3500)

Max and David's
8120 Old York Road, in the Yorktown Plaza, corner of Church Road. Kosher. Good spot for a meal when visiting either Keneseth Israel or Beth Sholom Synagogues on Old York Road, Elkins Park (215-885-2400)

National Museum of American Jewish History
Independence Mall, corner of Fifth and Market Streets

Philly Falafel

1740 Samson Street, between Seventeenth and Eighteenth Streets. Israeli (215-569-8999)

Seventeenth Street Felafel

A street corner stand on Seventeenth and Market Streets. Popular with the city lunch crowd. Lunch only and closed Shabbat (215-738-5732)

Shouk

622 South Sixth Street. Israeli (215-627-3344)

Zahav

237 St. James Place, a tiny street on the hill opposite the Bourse Theatre complex at Second and Walnut Streets. Israeli gourmet (215-625-8800)

BIBLIOGRAPHY

BOOKS

Auerbach, Jerold. *Rabbis and Lawyers: The Journey from Torah to Constitution*. Bloomington: Indiana University Press, 1990.

Blood, William. *Apostle of Reason: The Biography of Joseph Krauskoph*. Pittsburgh, PA: Dorrance and Company, 1973.

Chajes, J.H. *Between Worlds: Dybbuks, Exorcists and Early Modern Judaism*. Philadelphia: University of Pennsylvania Press, 2003.

Chametzky, Jules, John Flestiner, Hilene Flanzbaum and Kathryn Hellerstein. *Jewish American Literature*. New York: W.W. Norton, 2000.

Friedman, Murray, ed. *Jewish Life in Philadelphia 1830–1940*. Philadelphia, PA: Institute for Study of Human Issues, 1983.

Hochman, Anndee. *Rodeph Shalom: Two Centuries of Seeking Peace*. N.p.: privately published by Rodeph Shalom, 1995.

Morais, Henry Samuel. *The Jews of Philadelphia: Their History from the Earliest Settlements to the Present Time.* Philadelphia, PA: Levytype Company, 1894.

Roth, Cecil. *The Life of Menasseh ben Israel.* Philadelphia, PA: Jewish Publication Society, 1934.

Schwartz, Laurens R. *Jews and the American Revolution: Haym Salomon and Others.* Jefferson, NC: McFarland & Company, 1987.

Shappes, Morris, ed. *A Documentary History of the Jews of the United States, 1654–1875.* New York: Schocken, 1976.

Solomon, Susan G. *Louis I. Kahn's Jewish Architecture.* Waltham, MA: Brandeis University Press, 2002.

Sussman, Lance. *Isaac Leeser and the Making of American Judaism.* Detroit, MI: Wayne State University Press, 1995.

Wolf, Edwin, II, and Maxwell Whiteman. *The History of the Jews of Philadelphia from Colonial Times to the Age of Jackson.* Philadelphia, PA: Jewish Publication Society, 1956.

BOOKS FOR YOUNG READERS

Ambler, Jane Frances. *Haym Salomon: Patriot and Banker of the American Revolution.* New York: Rosen Publishing Group, 2004.

Fast, Howard. *Haym Salomon: Son of Liberty.* N.p.: self-published by Julian Messner, 1941.

Knight, Vick. *Send for Haym Salomon.* Vista, CA: Bordon Publishing, 1976.

Milgrim, Shirley. *Haym Salomon: Liberty's Son.* Philadelphia, PA: Jewish Publication Society, 1979.

ARTICLES

Katz, David S. "Edmund Gayton's Anti-Jewish Poem Addressed to Menasseh ben Israel, 1656." *Jewish Quarterly Review* 71, no. 4 (1981): 239–50.

Rosenbloom, Noah H. "Menasseh ben Israel and the Eternality of Punishment Issue." *Proceedings of the American Academy for Jewish Research* 60 (1994): 241–62.

Schorsch, Ismar. "From Messianism to Realpolitik: Menasseh ben Israel and the Readmission of the Jews to England." *Proceedings of the American Academy for Jewish Research* 45 (1978): 187–208.

PAMPHLETS

Trussel, John B.B., Jr. *William Penn: Architect of a Nation.* Harrisburg: Pennsylvania Historical and Museum Commission, 1998.

Vining, Elizabeth Gray. *William Penn: Mystic as Reflected in his Writings.* Pendle Hill Pamphlet 167. N.p.: Pendel Hill Publications, 1969.

INDEX

About the Author

Photograph by Beth Peckman.

Linda Nesvisky is a prize-winning artist, and her photographs have appeared in numerous publications. She studied art and art history at Carnegie Mellon University and the University of Pittsburgh and has a special interest in history and architecture. Linda has traveled throughout the world and, most notably, lived for many years in Israel. There she maintained an art studio in Jerusalem, taught at various schools and served as tour guide in the Old City's Jewish Quarter, where she lived in a restored thirteenth-century home. Today she maintains her studio in Philadelphia, where she also works as a city tour guide and runs ShalomPhillyTours for tours of Jewish interest. She is a member of Congregation Keneseth Israel, where she serves on the Adult Education Committee and is part of Temple Judea Museum's artist cooperative.

YOU MIGHT ALSO ENJOY

HISTORIC SYNAGOGUES
OF PHILADELPHIA & THE
DELAWARE VALLEY

Julian H. Preisler

978.1.59629.572.8

6 x 9 * 128pp * $19.99

In 1740, Nathan Levy—one of the first Jewish residents of Philadelphia—requested a plot of land to give his child a Jewish burial. This plot on Spruce Street became the first Jewish communal cemetery and marked the beginning of organized Jewish life in the colonial city. Throughout the nineteenth century, floods of Czech and German immigrants poured into Jewish communities and Reform and Orthodox synagogues began to spring up throughout the Delaware Valley. Today, Philadelphia's myriad synagogues are like living museums of architectural history. From small wooden structures that evoke Eastern Europe to the sharp angles, modern lines and soaring Sanctuary space envisioned by Frank Lloyd Wright, these synagogues reflect changing trends in style, design and function. With this comprehensive collection of images, Preisler helps record the region's unique religious and cultural history and captures in time its architectural treasures.

Visit us at
www.historypress.net